Carlo Mont

BOTTICELLI

art courses

ATS Italia Editrice

Contents

Right:
Self-portrait of Sandro Botticelli in the *Adoration of the Magi* (detail)
Florence, Galleria degli Uffizi

"Sandro di Botticello, most excellent artist, both on panel and wall; his works have a virile air and they possess perfect reason and complete proportion."

(Letter to Ludovico il Moro from an agent sent to Florence, c. 1485)

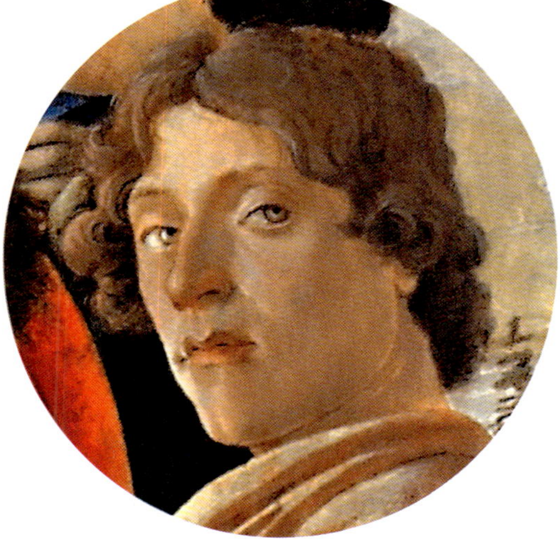

Botticelli, or the ideal beauty

Alessandro Filipepi, better known as Sandro Botticelli, was born in Florence in 1445 to Mariano di Vanni di Amedeo, a tanner, and Smeralda. According to the stereotype which attributes poor health to the children of elderly parents – his father was 52, his mother 40 – pretty old for the time – he was "sickly": or at least his father says he is in the buildings registrar of February 28 1458, adding the phrase "sta allegere". The meaning of this verb has been questioned, since the obvious reading "a leggere" (he is studying) could be a spelling error for "a legare" (to set precious stones). Herbert Horne doesn't agree, noting that "legare" would have been written as *leghare* in that time. Either way, we know for a fact that one of Sandro's three older brothers, Antonio, was a goldsmith, or more specifically a "battiloro", which comes from "batter l'oro", literally, a beater of gold. This was the precise work of reducing the precious and highly malleable metal into leaves of an impalpable thinness, in order to apply them to the wooden frames of paintings, and to paintings themselves, perhaps to illustrate the halos of saints, decorate the clothes of important people, or illuminate objects. In Florence, a "battiloro" was also called a "battigello". It's probable that Sandro "del battigello", of the "battigello", rapidly became Botticello and then Botticelli, in a common corruption. Vasari thinks differently, believing that Sandro as a boy had trained in a workshop belonging to a friend of his father's who was a goldsmith, known as Botticello for the usual reasons. In any case, the future painter was introduced to the goldsmith's art, as we can tell not least from his repeatedly demonstrated aptitude for enriching his masterpieces with the application of gold. Working as a goldsmith includes the art of design; it is hardly a coincidence that 70 years before, Filippo Brunelleschi had enjoyed a similar experience with incredible profit. The talent of Sandro was certainly noticed, as half way through the 1470s he turns up in the workshop of Filippo Lippi in Prato. We can't exclude the hypothesis that it was the Vespucci family that introduced him to the painter priest, an influential clan which lived in Borgo Ognissanti, near the Filipepis. This latter family, originally from the Santa Croce district, had moved in 1433 to Santa Maria Novella. For the time, it was a considerable shift. Later, the family changed districts again: first to Via delle Vigna Nuova, then to Via Nuova (today Via del Porcellana), a street running across Ognissanti in which the eld-

erly Mariano, now retired, bought a home. Born in Borgo Ognissanti, Sandro established his workshop in his paternal neighbourhood and lived there until his death. It would have been a life spent locally, typical of the cities (at the time, Florence was the second largest city in Europe after Paris), which also had repercussions on the work of Botticelli. The "Medici" *Adoration of the Magi* and *Nativity* were set in Santa Maria Novella: the *St Augustine in his Cell* in the church of Ognissanti; the *Annuciation* in the hospital of Santa Maria della Scala; the *Deposition* in the church of San Paolino; the backboard with *Venus and Mars* in the house of the Vespucci family: in fact, all the places in which these works of Sandro's were painted or set were located within 500 metres of one another...
Returning to the story, we know very little about the young man's stay in Prato; Filippo Lippi had already moved to Spoleto by 1467 with his son Filippino, where he would die two years later. On his return to Florence, Sandro spent some time in the studio of Il Verrocchio and that of del Pollaiolo; not exactly as a pupil, but rather as a professional collaborator, seeing as the historian Benedetto Dei mentions him as the owner of the workshop in 1470. In the same year, his growing prestige led the way for some important commissions from significant magistrates: the *Madonna del Roseto* for the powerful Guild of Wool; the backboard of *Fortitude* for the Mercantile court, who on that occasion preferred him over Piero del Pollaiolo. Two years later, he became a member of the company of Saint Luke, thus entering officially into the society of Florentine painters. Beside his name we find, as an apprentice, the name of Filippino Lippo, who was 15 at the time: having come to Florence after the death of his father, he would work at Botticelli's side for many years.
The fame of "Sandro Botticelli, painter" progressed "abroad" between 1474 and 1475 and on more than one occasion in Pisa, where he first reached an agreement with the Wardens of the Cathedral and then produced the now lost fresco the *Assumption of Mary* for the chapel of the Incoronata. But this period also marks the beginning of a particularly long and fruitful relationship with the Medici family and the intellectual circles that attended their homes in Via Larga. During the tournament held in Piazza Santa Croce on January 29, 1475, the brother of Lorenzo the Magnificent, Giuliano, would carry a banner featuring *Pallas armed*, designed by Poliziano and executed by Botticelli; we can also presume that a few months later the artist's *Adoration of the Magi* was placed in the Lami chapel of Santa Maria Novella, in which the artist depicts himself in full figure along with members of the family, living and dead, as well as the humanists which were allied with the Medici clan. Under the standard of the Medici family, Sandro was employed for almost twenty years in such a central role as to inspire the description "artist of the regime." In 1478, after the conspiracy of the Pazzi had been foiled, in which Giuliano had died, the Signoria, which was controlled by the Medici family, instructed the painter to portray the conspirators (hanged by the neck if brought to justice, hung by one foot if they had been fugitives) in the Palazzo Vecchio, on the door of the Dogana. But for the mentality of the time it was a contract like any other, although, when the building was restored in 1494 and the frescoes vanished, Sandro would not mind at all. Of greater interest is another matter: whether in the great allegorical works such as *Primavera*, the *Birth of Venus* and *Pallas and the Centaur* - the realisation of which marks a watershed in 1481 with the splendid group of frescoes in the Sistine Chapel - the artist limited himself to creating images

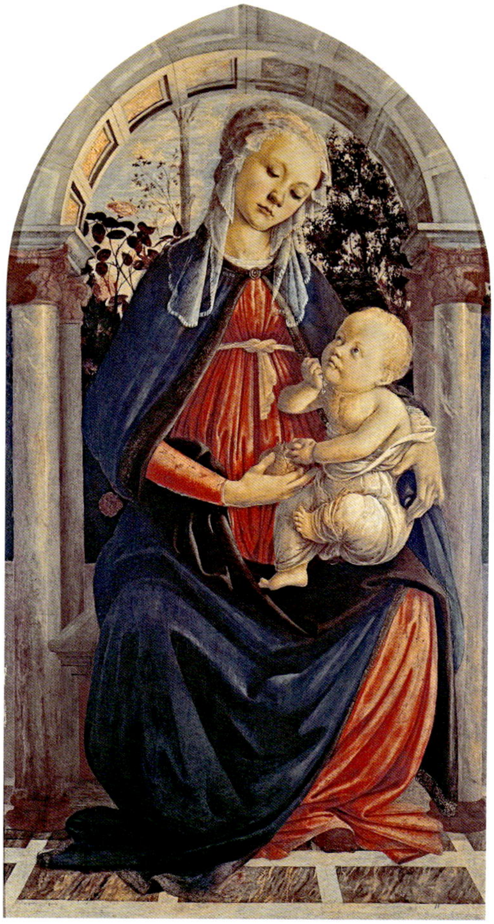

Madonna of the Rose Garden, Galleria degli Uffizi, Florence from a given iconographic programme dictated by a humanistic environment, or participated personally in their elaboration. Vasari – whose narration of the life of Botticelli includes not only marginal inaccuracies - suggests the painter has a rather odd intelligence and describes him as a man "without letters". But a number of indications suggest otherwise. If he had been deprived of education, intellectual curiosity and involvement, Sandro would not have been so passionately devoted to the study and execution of the *Divine Comedy*, on which he spends the time and the effort that indeed Vasari rather meanly reproaches him for. The drawings, in fact, that he carries out to illustrate the poem are full of reflection and a deep love. Another indirect proof of intellectual effort is his long meditation that begins towards the end of the life of il Magnifico, inspired by the preaching and works of Savonarola, which continues through the nineties and ends up materialising in a new form, based on the recovery and reinterpretation of Gothic art and a very personal interpretation of the values of perspective. Works such as the *Deposition* kept today in the Poldi Pezzoli museum and in Munich, and in particular the *Nativity* conserved in London, considered sometimes rather convoluted with respect to the "golden age" of the fifteen year period 1474-1490, actually show in their mystic qualities a deliberate compositional quest. Sandro Botticelli died in 1510. For some time the art of painting had taken a very different path; and if Vasari's affirmation, that the artist spent his final years in desolate poverty, is once again false, it effectively symbolises the plight of the artist who outlives himself. After that the figure of the master sinks into the oblivion of centuries. To perceive its return, we must wait until the second half of the nineteenth century, when Ruskin and the Pre-Raphaelite English – although with notable ambiguities in interpretation – bring a new attention to his work. Then, at the dawn of the twentieth century, Herbert Horne creates a monumental biography which opens a new chapter on Botticelli, and is still definitive today in many respects. Nowadays *Primavera* and the *Birth of Venus*, like Michelangelo's *David*, have become objects of mass worship. Although not all the issues relating to their allegorical meaning or, more generally, those concerning the authenticity and dating of many of his other paintings have been resolved, the hard work of scholars, supported by diagnostic tests and restoration campaigns, has already been and will undoubtedly continue to prove prodigious in terms of new revelations and discoveries.

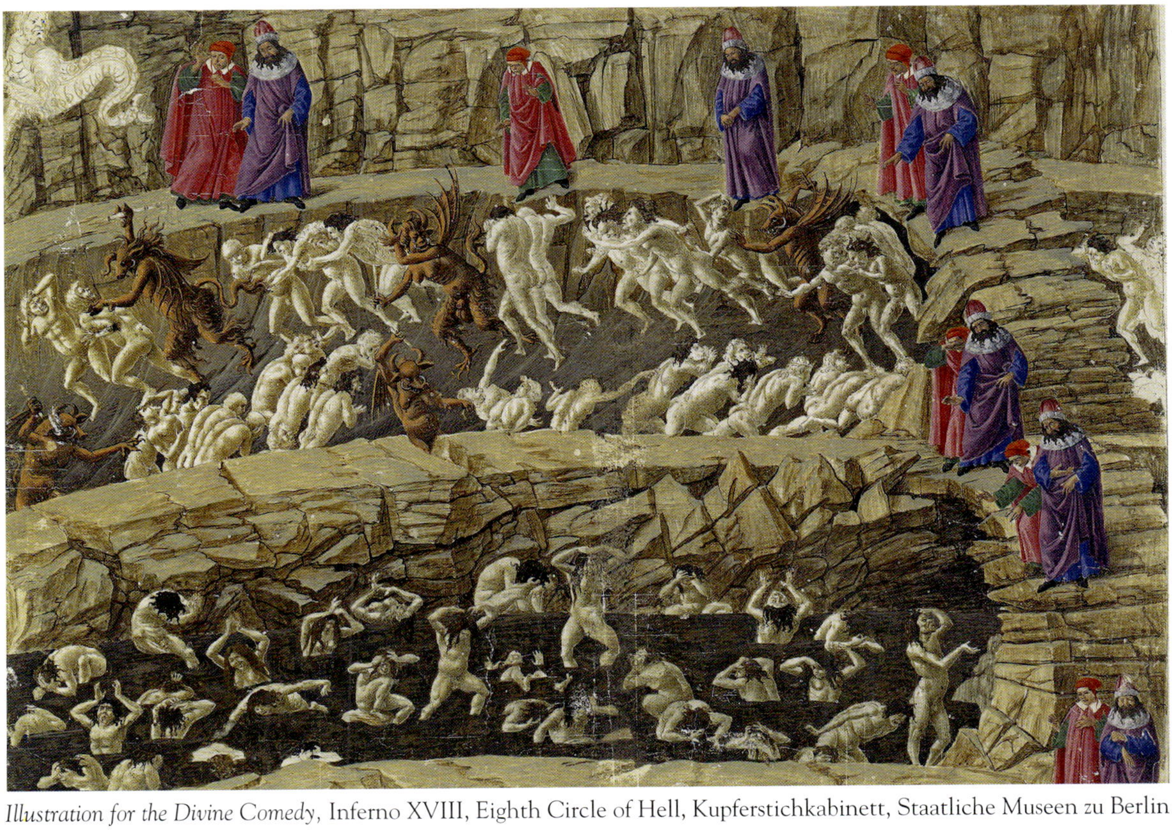

Illustration for the Divine Comedy, Inferno XVIII, Eighth Circle of Hell, Kupferstichkabinett, Staatliche Museen zu Berlin

Florence
Galleria degli Uffizi

Fortitude
1470, tempera on shaped panel, 167 x 87 cm

In order to settle disputes between merchants, the Mercantile court was established in Florence, consisting of six elected representatives of the *Arti Maggiori* or Major "Trades" and chaired by a consul. The tribunal resided for a long time in a building of the same name (1359), located between Piazza della Signoria and Via de 'Gondi. In 1469 it was decided to decorate the wall behind the benches of the judges with seven paintings depicting the *capital Virtues*. When the Uffizi palace was erected, the court was placed on the ground floor of the new building (1572). In 1770 the Grand Duke Peter Leopold decreed the abolition of the Trades and the paintings ended up in storage, from which they emerged in 1861 to be exhibited in the Uffizi.
Strictly speaking, the allegory of *Fortitude* shouldn't have fallen to Sandro: in fact on December 18, 1469, the Mercantile consul had allotted all the virtues to Piero del Pollaiolo. In the end however the subsequent consul, Tommaso Soderini - probably disappointed with the first few results - asked Verrocchio to produce a test drawing, and then, in May 1470, commissioned two *Virtues* from Sandro. On June 18, the twenty five year-old artist was officially confirmed for the job, and by August 18 had already been paid for *Fortitude*, which demonstrates the rapidity of its execution. The second planned *Virtue* was passed back to Piero, however, who in the meantime had probably made known his grievances.
The first documented work by Botticelli, *Fortitude* reflects the image of an artist still looking for direction. Knowing that he couldn't veer from the overall plan for the other Virtues, the design reveals strong Pollaiolo influences, even if not from Piero but rather his brother Antonio, a distinguished sculptor and designer, who provided some sketches and drawings to his less skilled relative. On the other hand, the young artist attempts to combine relief and movement typical of Antonio with the delicate beauty of his master Filippo Lippi, but the marriage is not very convincing. However, there are some characteristics which mark the future evolution of Sandro, in particular the treatment of the drapery and the colour scheme of three tones (in this case white, purple and blue). Interestingly, from a technical point of view, it is the depiction of gold, in decorations and metals, which attests to his apprenticeship as a goldsmith; in terms of costume, the styling of the hair, which hangs down from the shoulders in two thick braids which meet between the breasts, follows a motif destined to return to the central figure in *Primavera* and the Venus of *Venus and Mars*.

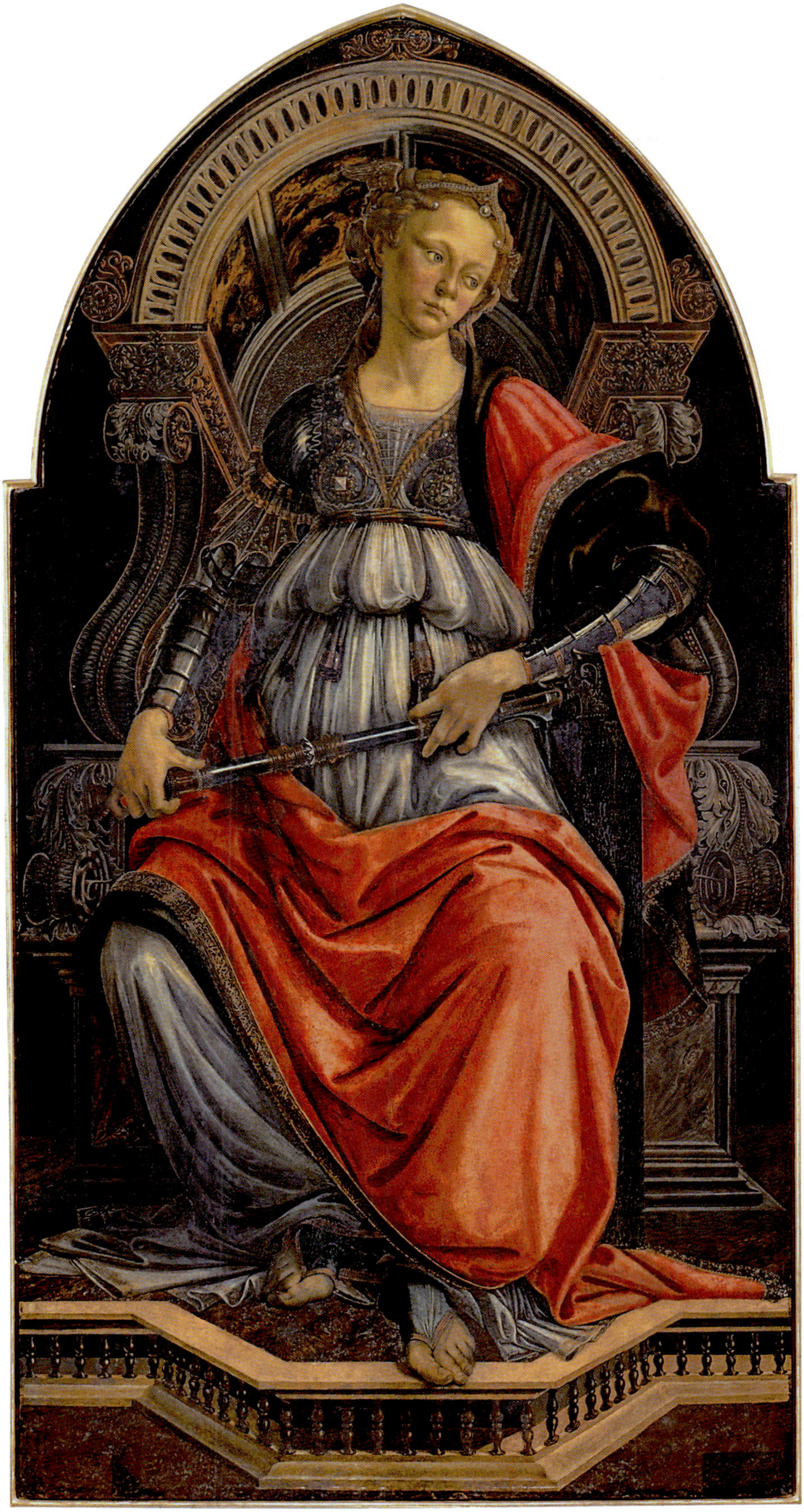

THE DIPTYCH OF JUDITH

We know nothing of the circumstances in which these two panels were executed or how they passed to their first known owner, sculptor Ridolfo Sirigatti, the master of Gian Lorenzo Bernini. The Sirigatti family had a workshop in Florence and enjoyed excellent favour at the court of the Medici, if we are to believe that in 1581 he was made a Knight of Justice of the military order of St. Stephen, established by Cosimo I to grant a noble title to "worthy" leaders of the affluent middle classes. In 1580 the sculptor donated these small paintings to Bianca Cappello, who for some years had been the second wife of Grand Duke Francesco, Cosimo's son, after having been his lover for a long period of time.

Ignoring whoever took the initiative to frame these two works together, they went on to end up in storage along with other paintings and antique statues. On the simultaneous death (by poisoning it seems) of Bianca and the Grand Duke, they were inherited by their only son Antonio de 'Medici, Prince of Capistrano. On his death in 1632, they were separated and placed side by side in the Tribuna degli Uffizi.

The panels depict, in close succession, two moments from the biblical story of Judith, told in the Old Testament book that bears her name. The Assyrians led by Holofernes, commander in chief of the army of Nebuchadnezzar, lay siege to the city of Bethulia. Its inhabitants, exhausted by thirst and hunger, are about to surrender, when the beautiful and pious widow Judith, a distant descendant of the patriarch Jacob, goes with her maidservant to the enemy camp and, posing as a seer, predicts victory for Holofernes. The latter, struck by her beauty and her talent, keeps her with him. On the

The return of Judith to Bethulia, detail, Galleria degli Uffizi, Florence

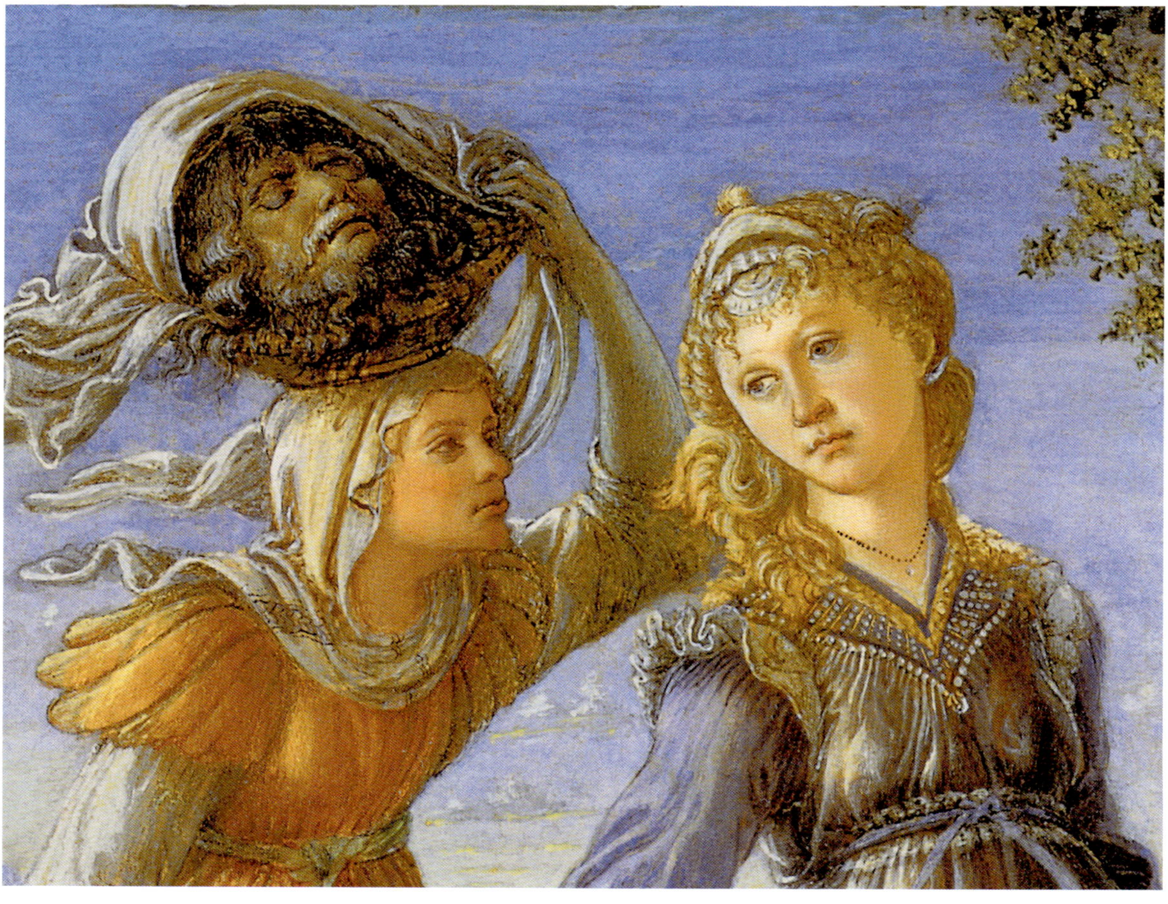

fourth day, the Assyrian general, eager to seduce her, invites her to dine with his trusted companion Bagoas. The exciting proximity of the young woman, however, induces Holofernes to drink more than he should, and when Bagoas and the other guests leave, convinced that the two will spend the night together, Judith beheads the sleeping General with his own sword and raises his head on the city walls. In the morning, Bagoas discovers the mutilated body in the tent of Holofernes: left without guidance, the besiegers panic and are massacred by the Jews.
Considered early works of Sandro, the two panels probably follow the allegory of *Fortitude* painted for the Mercantile court by a few years; indeed, the expression of Judith with its sweet melancholy recalls the face of *Fortitude* in many ways.
We should remember that according to a tradition which had been popular since the Middle Ages the biblical heroine was a symbol of virtue that opposes vice, and of chastity that contrasts lust. To this interpretation we must add and overlap that of the personification of civic virtue: it is no coincidence that the bronze depicting Judith and Holofernes, a masterpiece by the older Donatello, predates Botticelli's diptych by just two or three decades. It should be said, finally, that Sandro would return to the same theme many years later, in 1490, curiously presenting the intermediate scene to the two described here: in the *Judith and Holofernes* which is now at the Rijksmuseum in Amsterdam, Judith emerges from the tent brandishing a sword in her right hand and holding the head of the Assyrian leader in her left. The atmosphere is totally different there, however, characterised in that case by a vengeful notion of divine justice not so far from the preaching of Savonarola.

The discovery of the body of Holofernes, detail., Galleria degli Uffizi, Florence

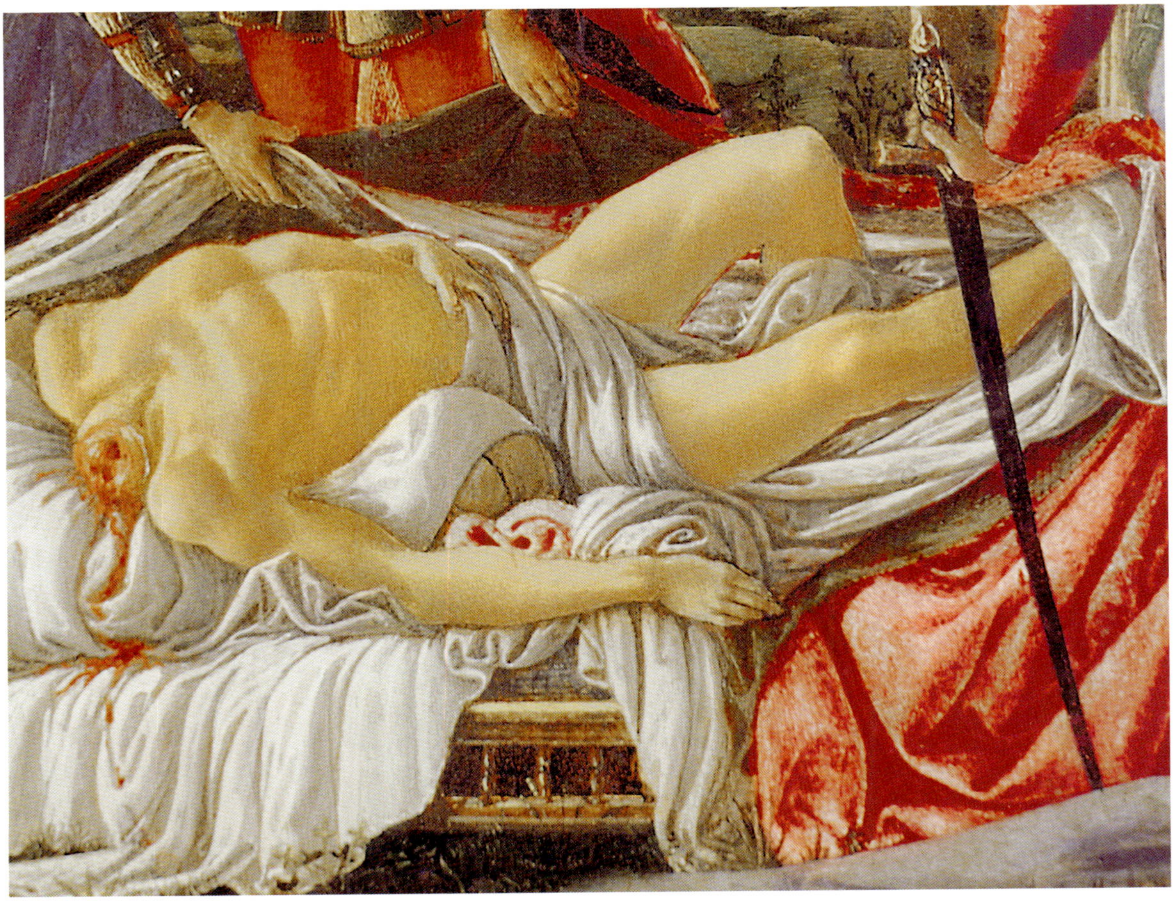

THE RETURN OF JUDITH TO BETHULIA,
c. 1472, tempera on panel, 31 x 24 cm

The painting depicts Judith who, leaving the Assyrian camp unnoticed, heads to Bethulia followed by her maidservant. This latter figure carries a basket on her head holding the Head of Holofernes, partly covered by a cloth. The heroine is still carrying the sword in her right hand with which she has killed the enemy general, while the left bears an olive branch, the symbol both of victory and peace in both in the Old Testament tradition (the dove of Noah, who returns to the ark with an olive branch in its beak: Gen. 8.11) and the Christian one (Olive or Palm Sunday). On the plain behind, closed by a line of hills, the walls of Bethulia stand to the right; in front of them a confused movement of horsemen perhaps alludes to the panic that is already taking over the Assyrian army after the news of the death of their leader.

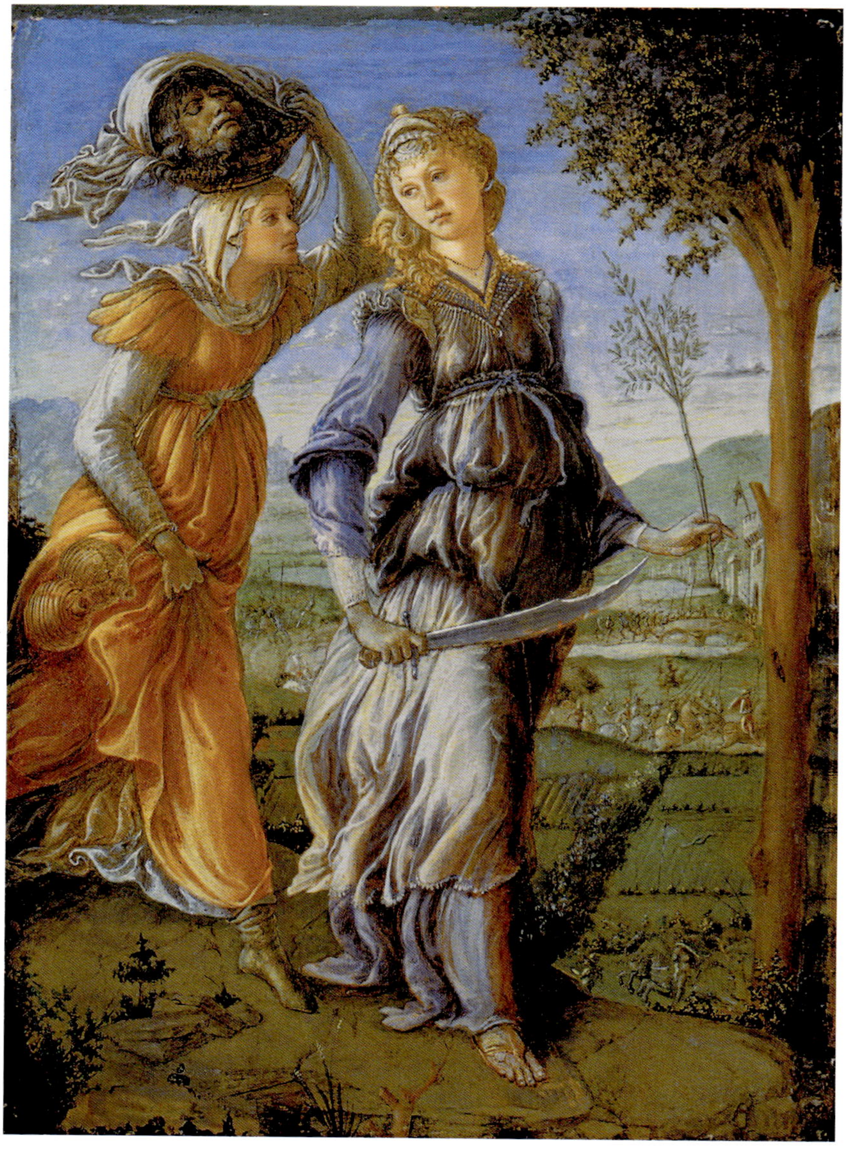

THE DISCOVERY OF THE BODY OF HOLOFERNES
c. 1472, tempera on panel, 31 x 25 cm

Composed in tones of white, red and blue, this picture, much darker than its predecessor, shows the discovery of the body of Holofernes. In constructing the scene the artist has allowed himself a bit more license compared to the biblical narrative: here, in fact, a crowd of dignitaries and lieutenants discover the corpse, not just Bagoas (perhaps identifiable as the central figure with the beard); furthermore, Holofernes lies in his own bed, and the gesture of the warrior bent in the foreground suggests that Judith has had to hide the body under the sheet and not, as stated in the Bible, pushed it to make him fall to the ground. In both cases this clearly falls to compositional needs, because on the one hand, the drama requires the "sounding board" of more than one spectator, and also because if the body of Holofernes is positioned on a lower level, those that discover him would have to bend down further, with a rather more flattening effect. Note the ingenious position of the knight, at the back of the group on the right; the curve of the neck of the horse continues in Bagoas' turban, in the right arm of the other dignitary and in that of the warrior in the foreground and creates, with the leg and right arm of the corpse, that circular motion that gives movement to the entire composition.

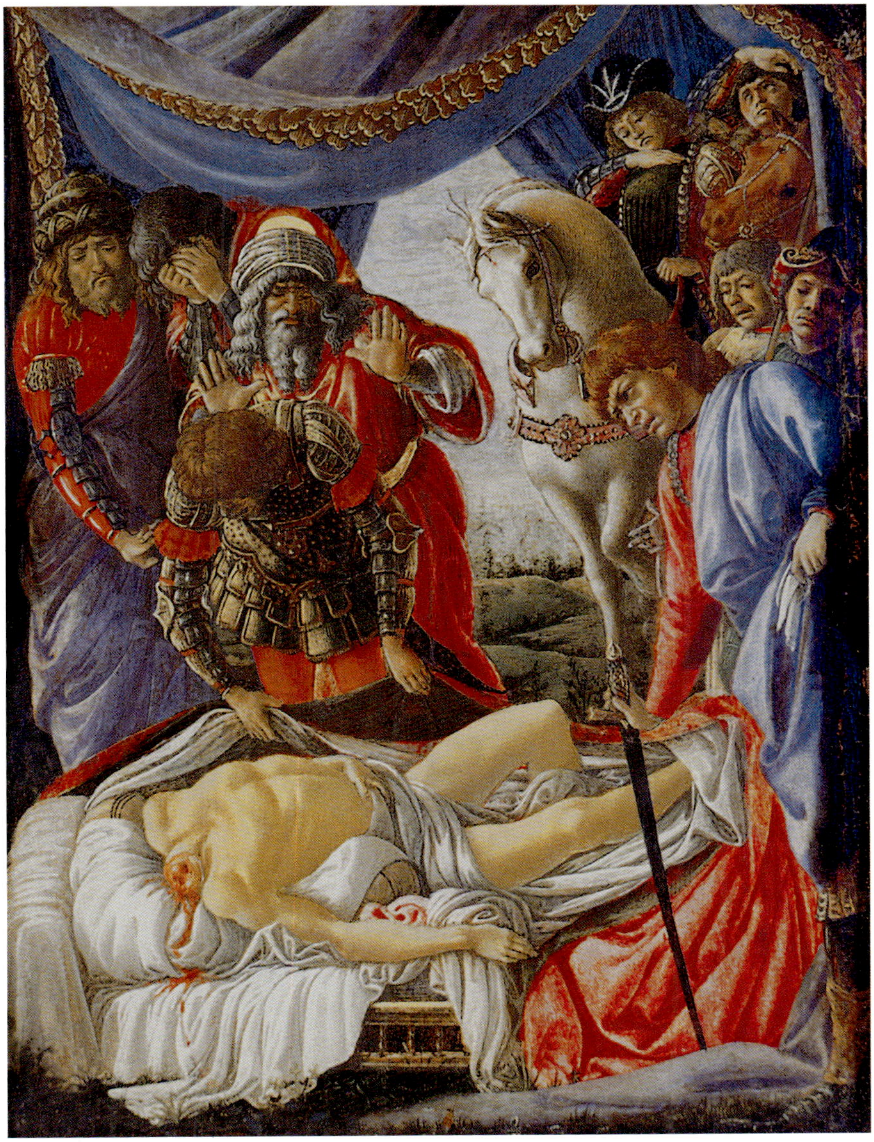

PORTRAIT OF A MAN WITH A MEDAL
C. 1475, tempera on panel, 57.5 x 44 cm

This work belonged to Cardinal Carlo de 'Medici, who died in 1666, bequeathing it to the Uffizi. The attribution to Botticelli dates to the end of the nineteenth century, and was then upheld by all later scholars.
The painting has two curious features: the frame is simply the moulding of the panel that acts as its support; in the bottom of the panel, in the middle, a circle has been cut in which a medal of gilded plaster has been inserted. Against the backdrop of a river landscape and a blue sky, veined by thin profiles of clouds, a young man with blue eyes, long bushy brown hair covered by a red cap (a "biretta"), wears a black robe with long sleeves; from the neck the hem of the white shirt sticks out, whose folds are created with an extraordinary realism. In his hands (and this is an absolute novelty for the portraiture of the time, which systematically "cut off" the arms) he holds the above-mentioned medal, bearing the profile of Cosimo the Elder surrounded by the script MAGNVS COSMVS • MEDICES PPP. It is indeed the cast of a medal actually coined between 1465 - when the Florentine republic distinguished Medici with the title of *Primus Pater Patriae*, "First Father of the Nation" - and 1469, when the same coin was reproduced for the first time in a miniature.
If, as we have said, there is no reason to doubt the attribution to Botticelli, the identity of the character portrayed remains a mystery. Those who have guessed at a member, legitimate or not, of the Medici family have had to (or rather, should have) retracted that idea in the face of chronogical facts, which also exclude the possibility of him being an intellectual close to the family, such as Pico della Mirandola. Its more likely that the figure is the actual creator of the coin, who has remained anonymous despite the fiercest research. Based on a piece of paper from the accounts of the Medicis and a facial analysis comparing it with the Botticellian self-portrait in *Adoration of the Magi*, it has been imaginatively assumed that the unknown goldsmith could be identifiable as Sandro's brother, Antonio, variously identified as a caster and gilder of medals. Again, however, we run into a chronological inconsistency because, at the time of the portrait, Antonio, born in 1430, should have been about forty years old.

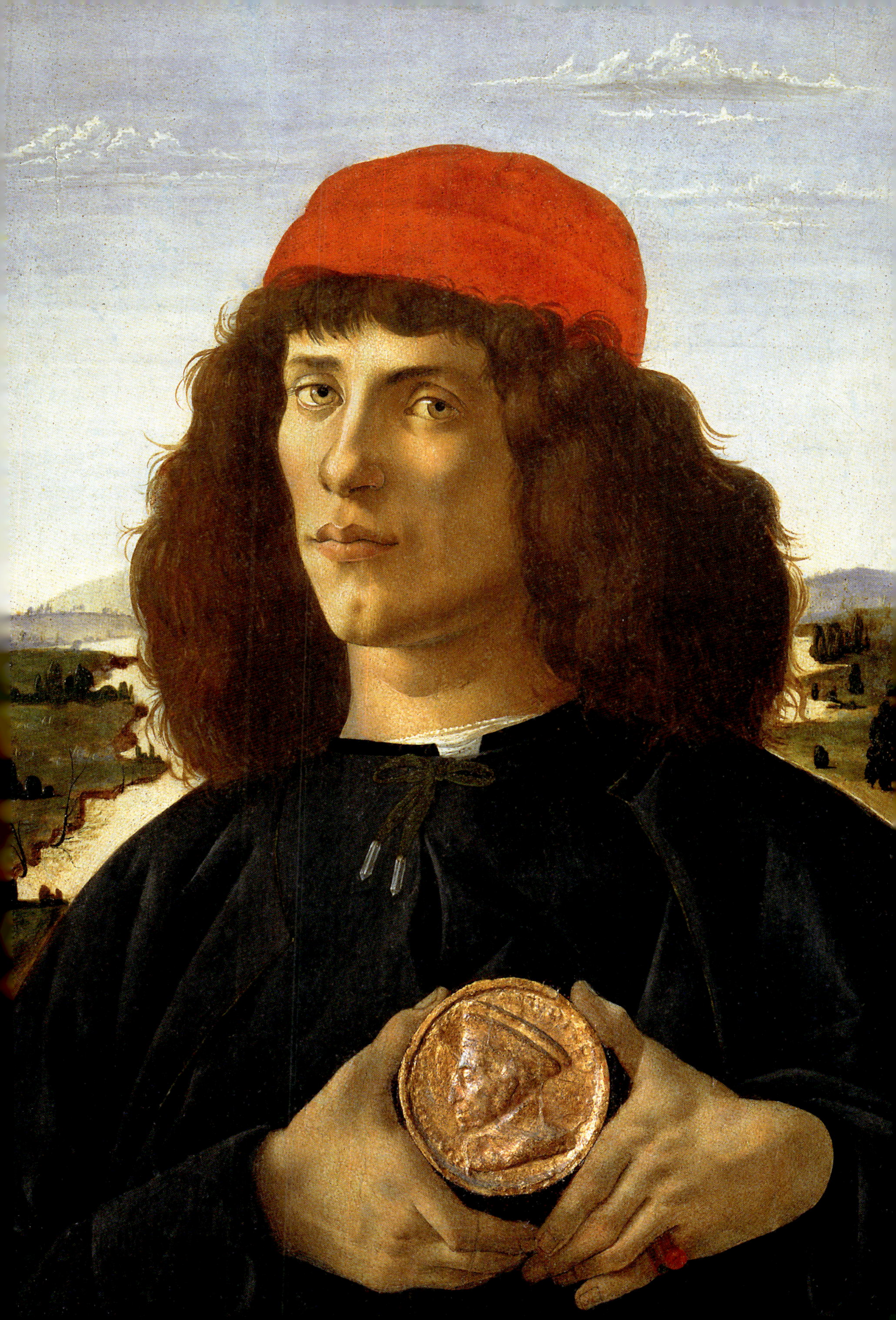

ADORATION OF THE MAGI
1475, tempera on panel, 111 x 134 cm

This work was located in Santa Maria Novella, according to ancient sources; in his Lives, Vasari gives it considerable praise. It was commissioned by Gaspare Lami, the son of a barber from Empoli, who had made his fortune in finance and maintained close relations with the Medicis in business and personal affairs. He held the patronage of an altar of the church which was dedicated to the Epiphany, because he had the same name as one of the Magi: hence the theme behind the picture destined to decorate the altar; a subject which, notes scholar Antonio Paolucci, "had been appropriated by the mythology of the Medicis for some time" and which had been used in 1459 by Benozzo Gozzoli for the chapel of their palace in Via Larga. The patronage of the altar later passed on, and the painting was sold to Bernard Vecchietti, who moved it to his own home, replacing it with an *Annunciation* by Santi di Tito. The *Adoration* appears later in the Villa del Poggio Imperiale, from where it was transferred to the Uffizi in 1796.
Besides the pictorial quality, the work is notable for the presence of dominant figures from the Medici family. At the time, the Medicis were still concealing their power play, refraining from taking major public offices: so, in suggesting to Sandro the subject of the panel, Lami was not moved by an explicit courtier's intent that might have contradicted the "minimalist" policies of the future rulers of Florence. Except that Cosimo, Piero and Giovanni de 'Medici were already dead, and the idea of portraying them as the Magi *post mortem*, i.e, as protagonists of that sacred story, would have jarred with contemporary thought, in as much as "the sanctification took place on the altar of a public chapel ... in a church governed by the Dominicans," guarded and guaranteed "by theological and liturgical orthodoxy" (Paolucci). We are, in fact, seeing the first objective signs of the construction of the family dynasty.
Along with the Medicis (il Magnifico is the young man on the left at the front) and their circle, the painter appears on the far right. He appears in bright relief, reflecting the prestige which he by now enjoyed from his patrons.
The Adoration of the Magi is a fundamental step in the art of Sandro, who, having assimilated the lessons of Antonio del Pollaiolo, has now found his own way. Remains of "some fanciful fluidity" (Mandel), such as the execution of the trees and the boat in the landscape of the far right, would disappear by the time he painted *Primavera*.

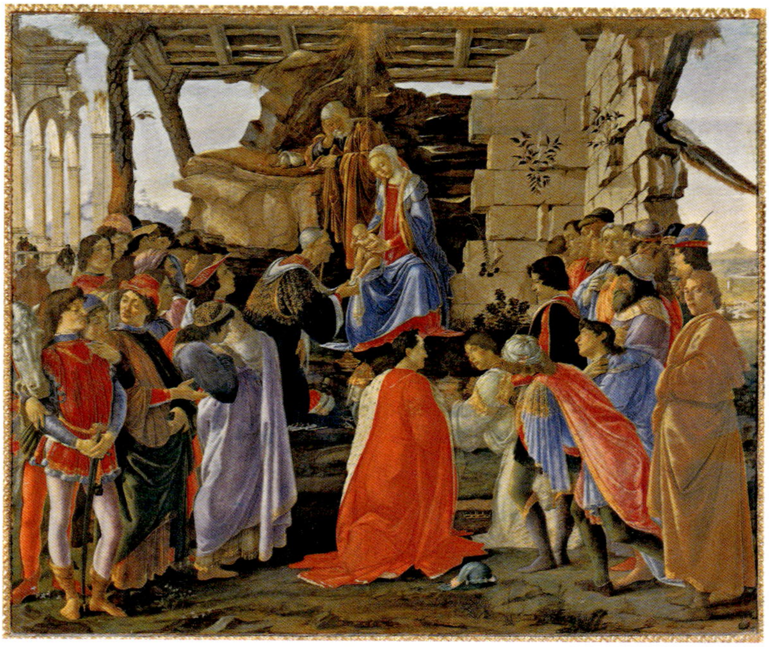

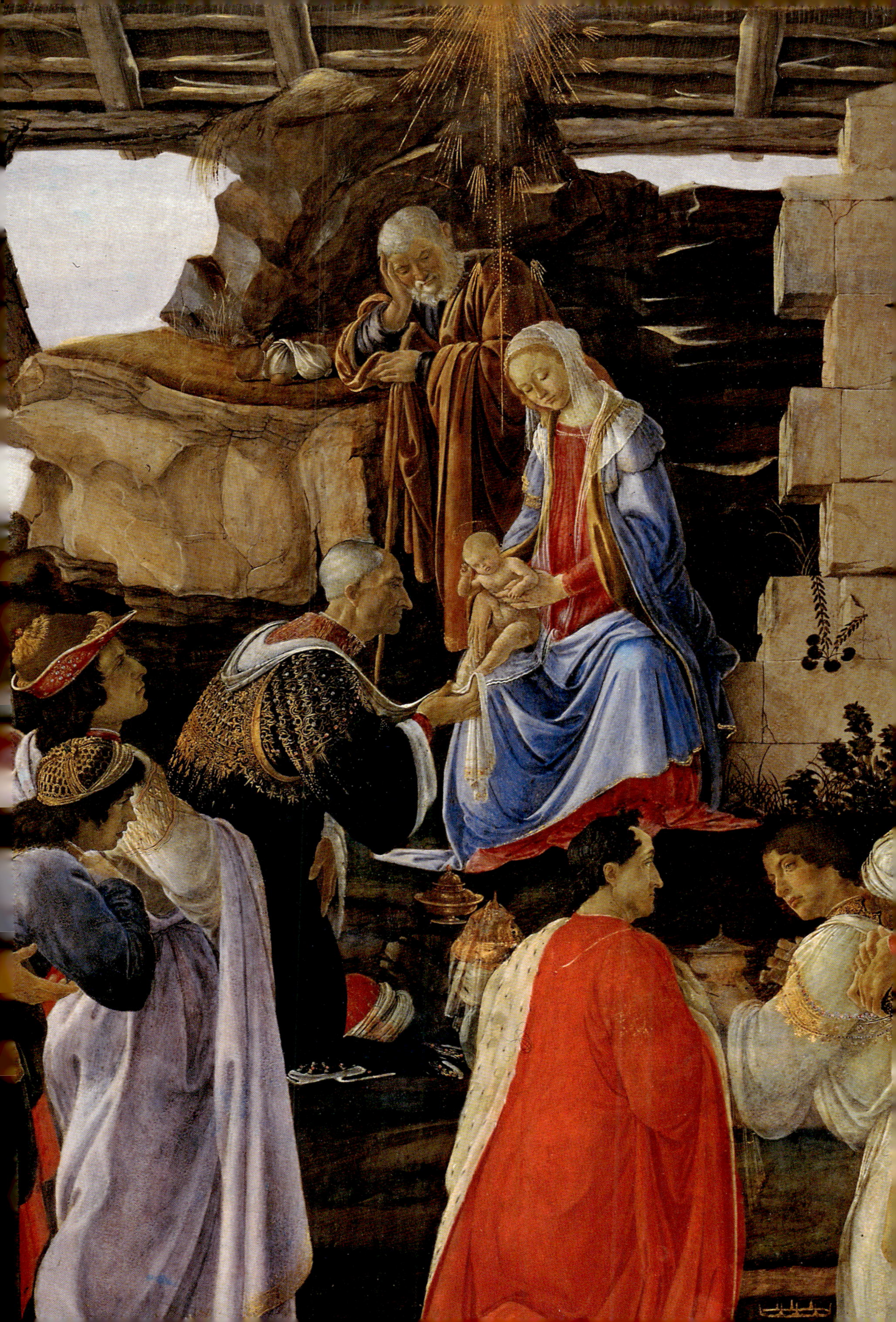

MADONNA OF THE MAGNIFICAT
1481, tempera on panel, ∅ 118 cm

This work reached the Uffizi via a private party, Ottavio Magherini, who sold it to the gallery in 1784. Its attribution to Botticelli, which was made for the first time in 1864 by Cavalcaselle, has never been seriously contested, although its dating oscillates between 1481 and 1485.
The entire composition follows the curving lines of its base and is framed by an unusual round window, through which we glimpse a fragment of countryside.
In the foreground on the right are positioned the Virgin and Child; in her left hand, the Madonna holds a pomegranate – symbol of resurrection – on which Jesus rests one hand. On the far right an angel, with a raised arm, holds a diaphanous crown of stars over the head of the Virgin, above which a halo hovers, symbolising the Holy Spirit; a second angel, showing only his face in profile, makes an identical gesture on the far left. Before him there are three more angels: the one in the foreground, seen in profile, is on his knees and holds an inkpot in his right hand, while his left holds a book open in which the Virgin, who is dipping in her pen, is about to write; the second, seen almost face on, watches the first thoughtfully; the third, standing behind them, raises his head slightly to see the book better.
On the right hand page of the volume is written the start of the *Magnificat*, from which the work has taken its current title, while on the left we can see the Song of Zachariah, which presages the birth of St John the Baptist, patron of Florence; therefore indicating a local sponsor. The imaginative suggestion that we are looking at a back-dated family portrait has little support: the Virgin is said to be Lucrezia Tornabuoni, wife of Piero de' Medici, with their children (in the foreground Lorenzo il Magnifico and Giuliano; behind, standing, Maria; Bianca and Nannina hold up the crown; the youngest, Lucrezia, would be the actual Child).
As far as the compositional aspect goes, it's worth underlining the artist's knowledge of movement, which includes the exquisite winding river in the scenery behind and the meeting of the hand of the Madonna with that of the angel, even if "the rhythm isn't so pronounced and decorative as might seem at first view, but much more subtle and interwoven and complex, in that in following it one loses sight of the physical beauty of the figures and finds oneself caught in movement which has the harmony of the celestial spheres." (G.C. Argan).

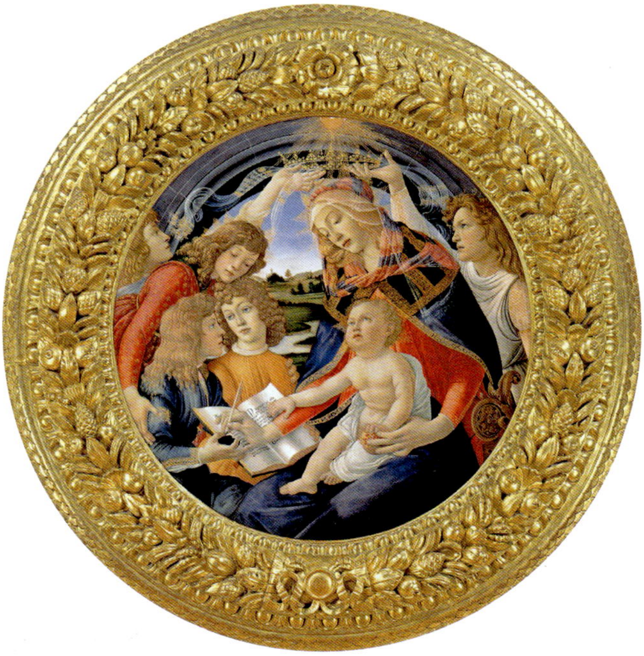

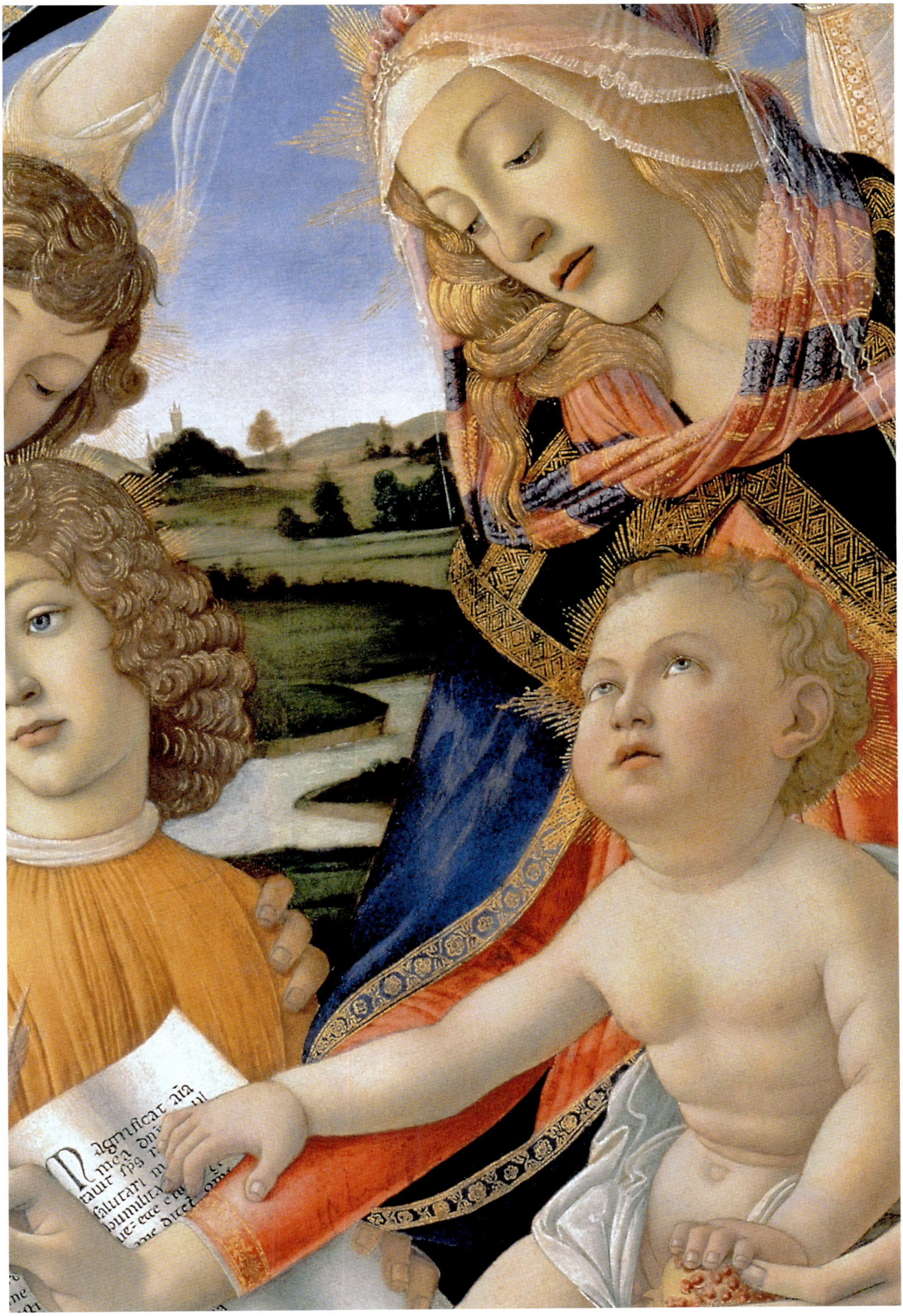

Primavera

1482, tempera on panel, 203 x 314 cm

This is today Botticelli's most famous work, and also his most enigmatic. Even the title, which was created by Vasari, lends itself to discussion because the Medici inventories also entitled it *Garden of Atlantis* or *Garden of the Hesperides*.

This great panel, along with *Pallas and the Centaur* and the *Birth of Venus* comes from the old house of the family in Via Larga, and its execution is credited to the same period as the other two paintings, i.e. slightly before or slightly after Sandro's stay in Rome. Perhaps commissioned by Lorenzo il Popolano and by Giovanni di Pierfrancesco, from a younger branch of the family, in 1537 Cosimo I moved it to the Villa di Castello, from where it emerged in 1815 to be hung in the Vasari corridor. In 1853 it was transferred to the gallery of the Academy, from where it made its definitive return to the Uffizi in 1919. The environment in which the scene takes place is a little flowering glade, closed in the background by an orange grove (although there are also other plants such as laurels, cypresses, a few conifers and another myrtle bush, which underlines the central figure). The backdrop of a uniformly blue sky contrasts with the intense green and brown tones of the vegetation which, like the figures, is illuminated with a soft and almost unreal light that casts no shadows. Furthermore, there is almost no sense of the weight of the figures, who almost seem to float above the grassy carpet.

The figures do not appear to be linked to one another by a narrative thread, thus denoting the purely allegorical purpose of the work. The problem is that of interpreting it: it's improbable composition, which has occupied generations of scholars, is still nowhere near being resolved. Although the subject of profound studies, the Florentine Renaissance itself is still far from yielding its vast secrets. It represents a complex cultural crucible, in which the broadest themes are mixed, from Neo-Platonism – in itself, a rich source of esotericism – to alchemy; from certain orthodox readings of the Christian message to a "science of nature", full of hints and symbolic references.

This work, conceived in esotericism and destined for those in the know, remains on the whole a mystery. It's defined as "an enigma" by the German scholar Edgar Wind, who laboured over it for many years.

We can, however, consider the traditional identification of the figures. From right to left, the first figure is

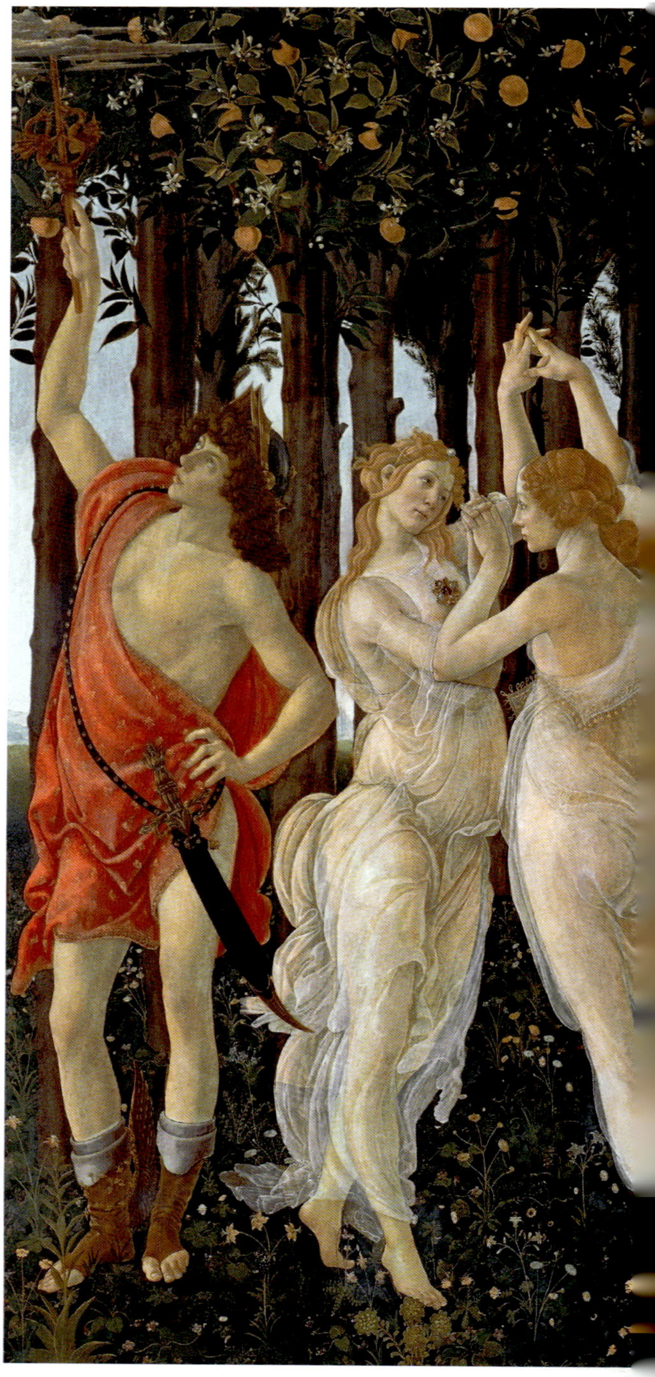

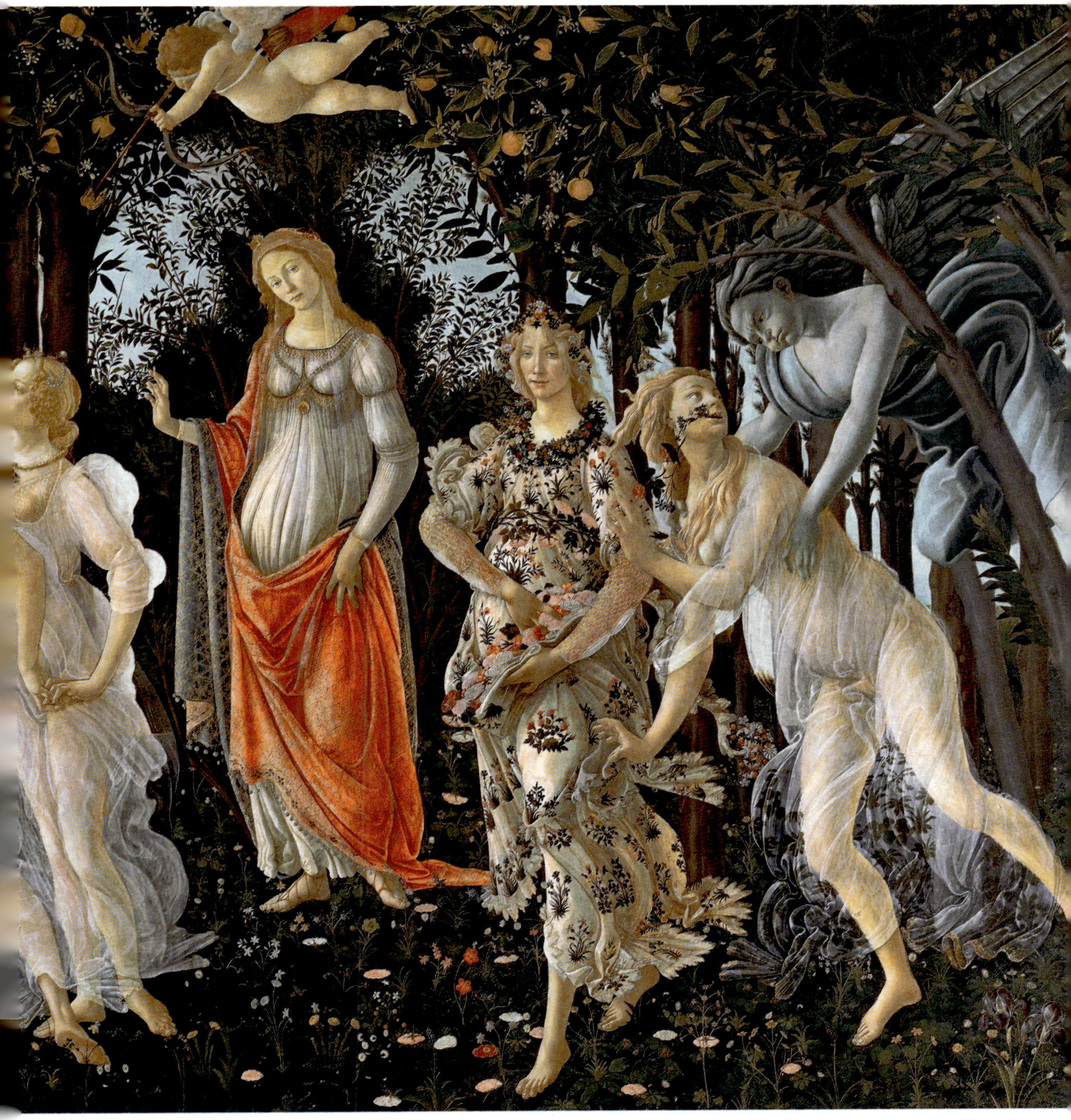

that of Zephyrus, the breeze of the spring. The god is caught in the act of carrying away the nymph Chloris (*chlorós*, "green"), who, according to Greek mythology, was responsible for making the plants verdant again, as we can see from the vines that come from

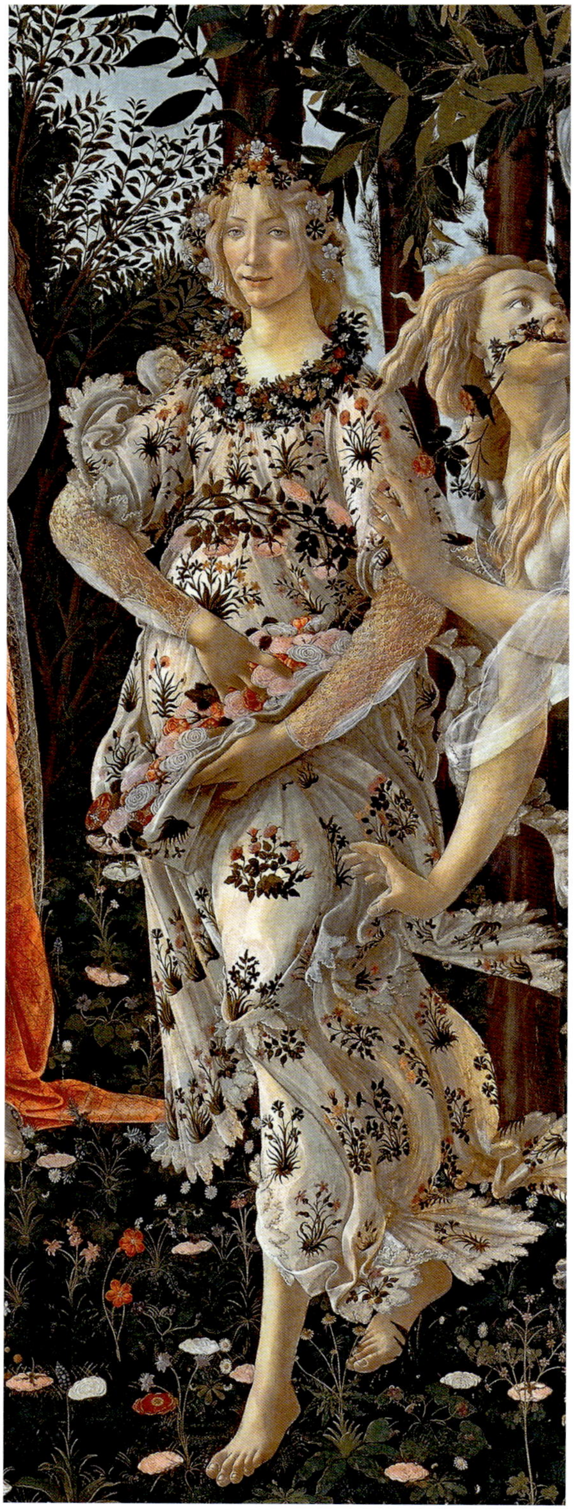

her mouth. The third figure is also Chloris, who, in line with a passage from Ovid's *Fasti*, is transformed into Flora, the goddess of the harvest and fertility, who is captured pulling flowers from her lap. At the centre of the composition, slightly upstage with respect to the other figures, is Venus against a background of myrtle, the plant which is consecrated in her name. Above we see Cupid, his eyes covered to symbolise love's blindness, pointing an arrow at the three dancing Graces; on the far left, Mercury scatters a blanket of clouds with his caduceus staff. The scenery, finally, recalls the details of the mysterious garden of the Hesperides; its golden apples were associated with citrus fruits in the Renaissance, a fruit which has since, by little coincidence, assumed the name of "hesperide". Coming to the various interpretations, these tend to always keep in consideration a vast resource of texts contemporary to the work (such as the *Stanze* and the *Rusticus* of Poliziano) or the ancient classics which were still well read and commented upon in Renaissance times (from Ovid's *Fasti* to the Golden Ass of Apuleius and to Lucretius' *De Rerum Natura*).

Returning to the Neo-Platonic theme, Gombrich (1985) cites a letter than Marsilio Ficino writes in 1477 to his pupil Lorenzo di Pierfrancesco to exhort him to follow Venus as a spiritual guide, allegory of the *Humanitas*, i.e. of humanist thought. If the central figure in the painting is Venus, the goddess of Love, we have before us an allegory from that intellectual discipline, which, distancing man from the call of the senses (symbolised by the triad of Zephyrus, Chloris and Flora) through reason (the Graces), elevates him towards contemplation (Mercury). A more recent approach (Villa, 1998) attributes the so-called *Primavera* with a completely different meaning. According to him, the work is a celebration of the rebirth of philology in the work of the circle of il Magnifico: the allegories in that case refer to the *De nuptiis Mercurii et Philologiae* ("The marriage of Mercury and Philology") of Martianus Capella (4-5 A.D.), an author read and admired in the Florentine Renaissance. Mercury (allegory of hermeneutics and eloquence) turns towards the sun (Apollo, god of poetry) to consult him on his marriage with Philology (instead of Venus). Favouring the unity are the three Graces, the spirit of Love and Rhetoric (instead of Flora); the nymph that flees from the winged spirit (the presumed Zephyrus) is Flora (and not Chloris), the protector of marriage vows.

There is also an interpretation with an historical / political slant (Acidini, 2001): the *Primavera* is celebrating the new flowering of Florence – *Florentia*, evoked by the figure of Flora – thanks to the Medicis; hence the oranges, which were known in Latin at the time as *mala medica*, "medicinal apples". Indeed, in the spring of 1480 il Magnifico, travelling in person to Naples to visit King Ferdinand of Aragon, manages to stop the war with that powerful sovereign and achieves the revocation of a papal interdict which had weighed heavily of Florence since the Pazzi plot (1478). It is precisely to this diplomatic event that we can credit the presence of Mercury, the god of mediation *par excellence*.

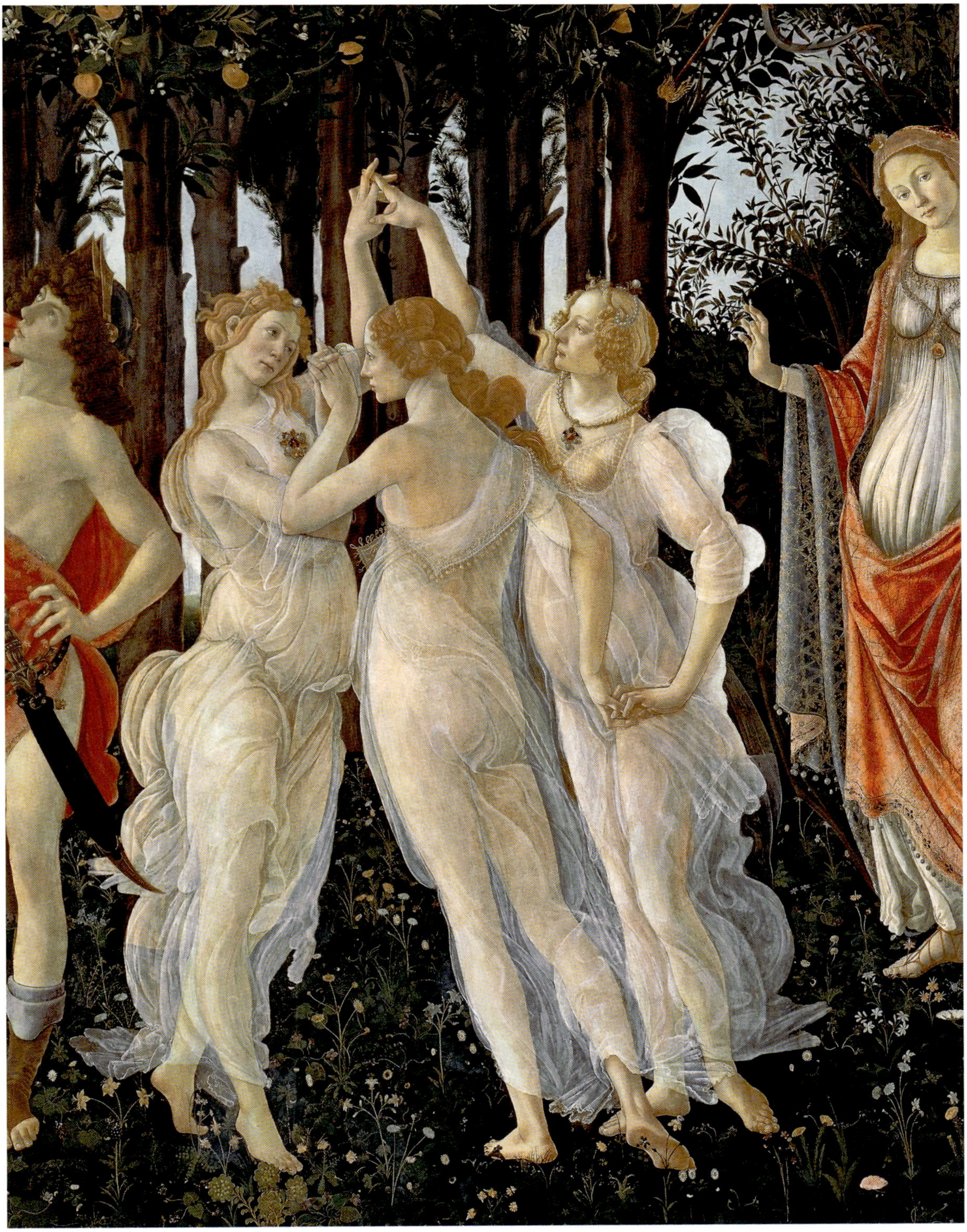

PALLAS AND THE CENTAUR
1482, tempera on canvas, 207 x 148 cm

This painting was originally hung in the old house on Via Larga (the present day Via Cavour), in a ground-level hall next to the room of Lorenzo il Popolano. In the inventory of his goods and of his brother Giovanni (1498-99) the subject of this work is identified as "Camilla and a Satyr", while in a later list (1516) "Minerva and the Centaur" is mentioned. Inherited by Giovanni delle Bande Nere, father of the future grand duke Cosimo I, it remained in the suburban villa at Castello until 1830, from where it was moved to Palazzo Pitti and later to the Uffizi (1922). The left hand side of the scene is filled with a wall of bare rock; its strata get progressively broader towards the top, to create almost a natural roof that at its apex fills almost two thirds of the breadth of the painting. Against the rock is a bearded centaur, with the appropriate attributes (a bow and quiver), who turns his head, with an almost pained expression, towards a young woman. She wears a long tunic of light tulle, patterned with a motif of three interlocking rings; a dark cloak hangs from her right shoulder to cover her waist. Her breast and her arms are covered with branches of evergreen, which also crown her head. The young woman holds a long wall halberd in her left hand, while with the right she grips a tuft of the long mane of the centaur. In the background, we see a maritime bay, with a ship coming into port. If the allegorical significance of the centaur seems unequivocal (since ancient times this mythological cross between a man and a horse has alluded to the untamed violence of instinct), identifying the female figure has been much trickier. The old inventory mentions Camilla, the virgin warrior and daughter of the Volsci, who in the Aeneid (l. XI, *passim*) perishes fighting against the Trojans; but the attributes that the girl has in the Botticellian painting are rather incongruous with those (bow, arrows, armour) of the Virgilian heroine. For the same reasons, the theory that she is Pallas (personification of the rationalism that beats instinct) also fails to hold up: she's missing the helmet, the aegis (the armour with the Medusa's head) and the lance. Much more convincing, in fact, are a few recent proposals, which are based on two considerations: a) that the symbol of the three interlocking rings belonged to the principal branch of the family, that of Cosimo il Vecchio and il Magnifico, and not to the younger brand of Lorenzo and Pierfrancesco; b) the evergreen which adorns the young woman is not olive, the symbol of peace, but myrtle, the symbol of Venus. The painting therefore would have been a gift from il Magnifico to his cousin of the same name, who fell under his protection amongst other things, on the occasion of his marriage with Semiramide Appiani, daughter of the Lord of Piombino (1482). There are conflicting views, however, on the significance of the allegory: according to Antonio Cecchi, it is "the primacy of the mind and the reason over the senses and earthly inclinations", with an indirect invite to not overlook the *studia humanitatis*; for Stanley Meltzoff, it refers to the chaste love which controls sensual passions: in this case, the invite would be particularly directed towards a proper marital life. An ancient source also serves to convalidate the identification of the girl with a chaste Venus. The sophist Athenaeus (II century A.D.) narrates how Herostratus, the faithful lover of Aphrodite, was caught up in a storm during a sea voyage. The goddess, invoked by him, appears in the form of a myrtle twig which shoots miraculously from the statuette before which Herostratus is praying. The miracle gives strength to the crew and the ship reaches a secure port. Herostratus then takes the statuette with the myrtle twig to the temple of Aphrodite, who from that point on becomes known as *naukràtis*, or "lady of the ships". In the light of the anecdote, the background of this painting with the ship that returns to port is perhaps much more than a stereotype.

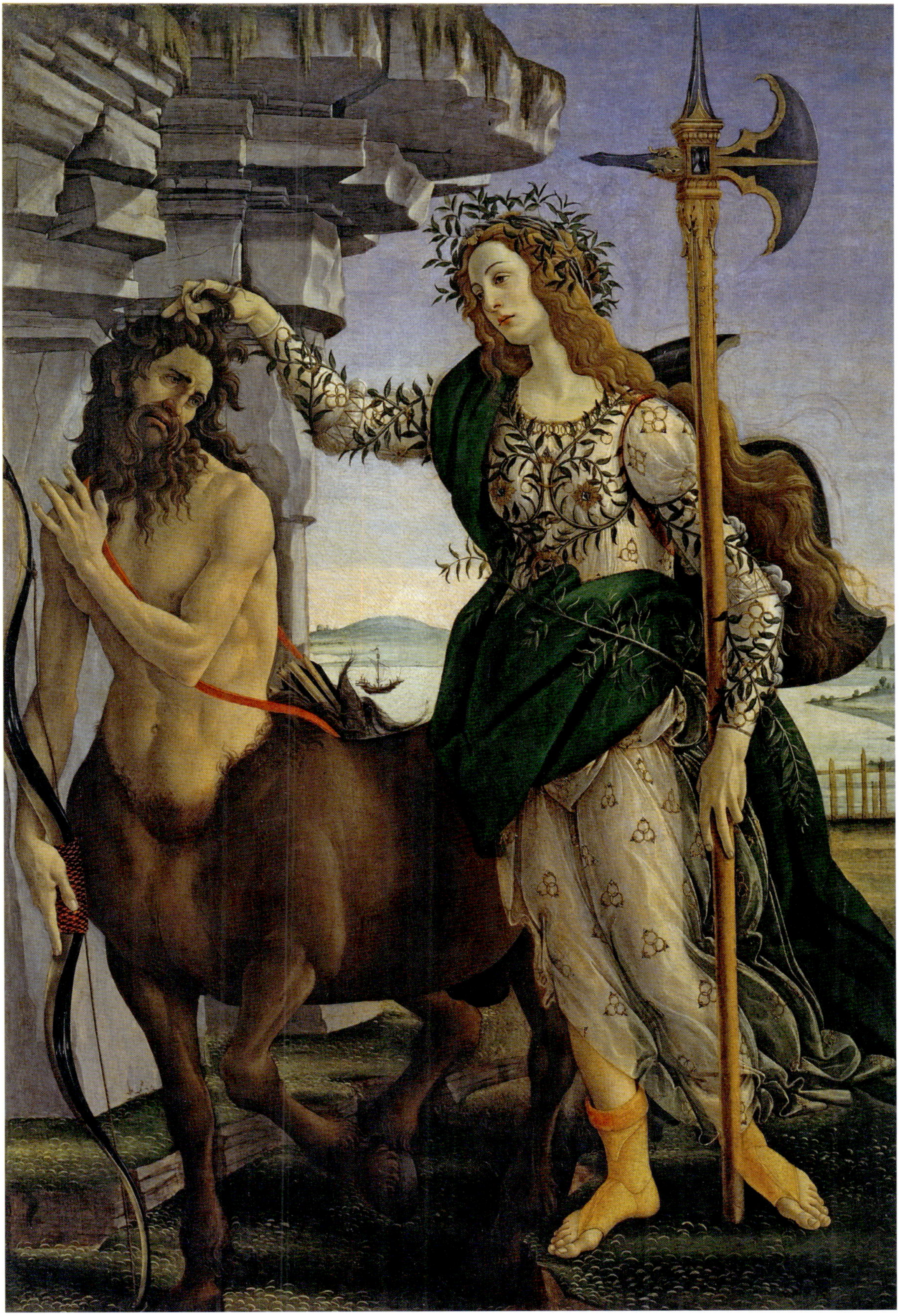

BIRTH OF VENUS

c. 1484, tempera on canvas nailed on to panel
172.5 x 278.5 cm

Like *Primavera* and *Pallas and the Centaur*, this *Birth of Venus* which was originally kept in the old house in Via Larga belonged to Lorenzo and to Giovanni di Pierfrancesco de' Medici. Moved to the villa in Castello along with the other two works, it followed the same fate as the *Primavera* until 1815 when it was transferred to the Uffizi.

At the centre of the great canvas is nude Venus, her long mane of hair undone by the wind, standing on an enormous shell which is about to run aground on the shore, enclosed on the right by an orange grove. On the left, Zephyrus, in a tight embrace with his bride, the nymph Chloris, blows in the goddess's direction: shower of tiny roses rains from the couple. On the right, in the foreground against the outline of the wood, one of the Horae offers Venus a cloak covered in hyacinths.

The subject appears to derive from Greek and Latin sources: the so-called Homeric songs, Ovid, etc. that describe Venus as Anadyomene ("emerging from the waters") and include the detail of the Horae (here Thallo or Thalatte, the divinity of the spring flowering) who hands the cloak to the goddess. The theories of those – and there have been many – that see Venus arriving on the scene are not necessarily in conflict with the interpretations that place the accent on the Neo-Platonic implications of the painting (E.H. Gombrich, 1945; C.G. Argan, 1956).

In this case, Gombrich feels we are looking at an allegory of the birth of *Humanitas*, generated by Nature through her four elements (air, the breath of Zephyrus; water, the sea; earth, the shore; fire,

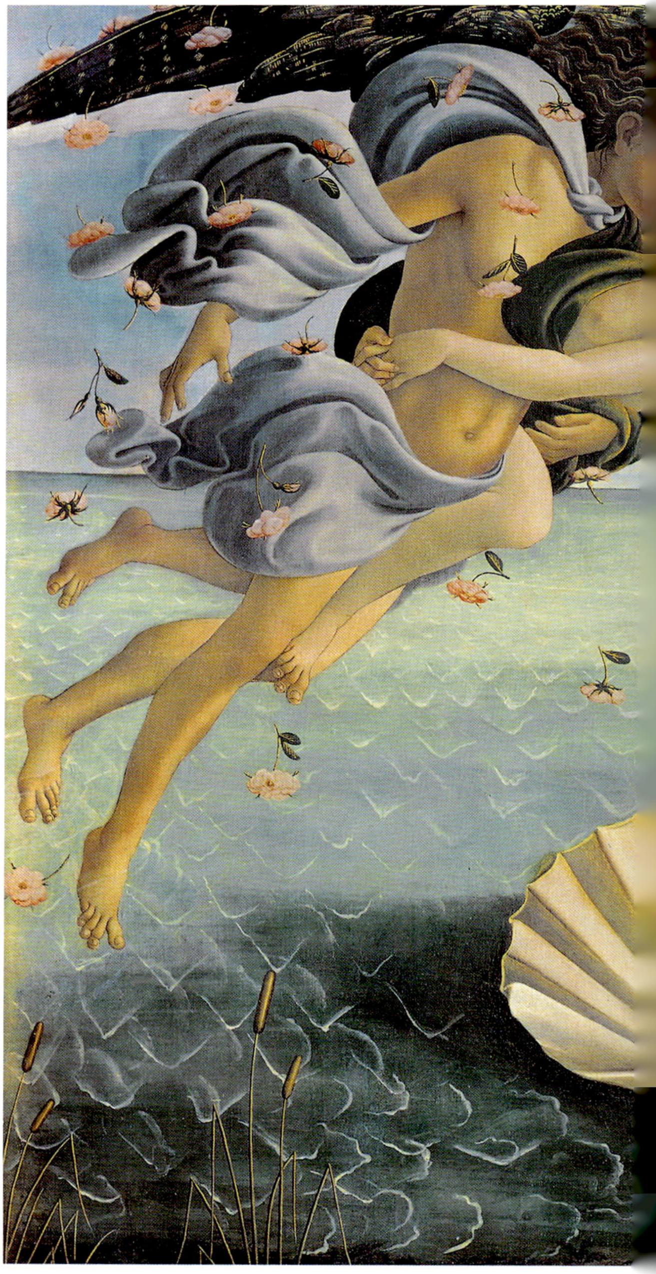

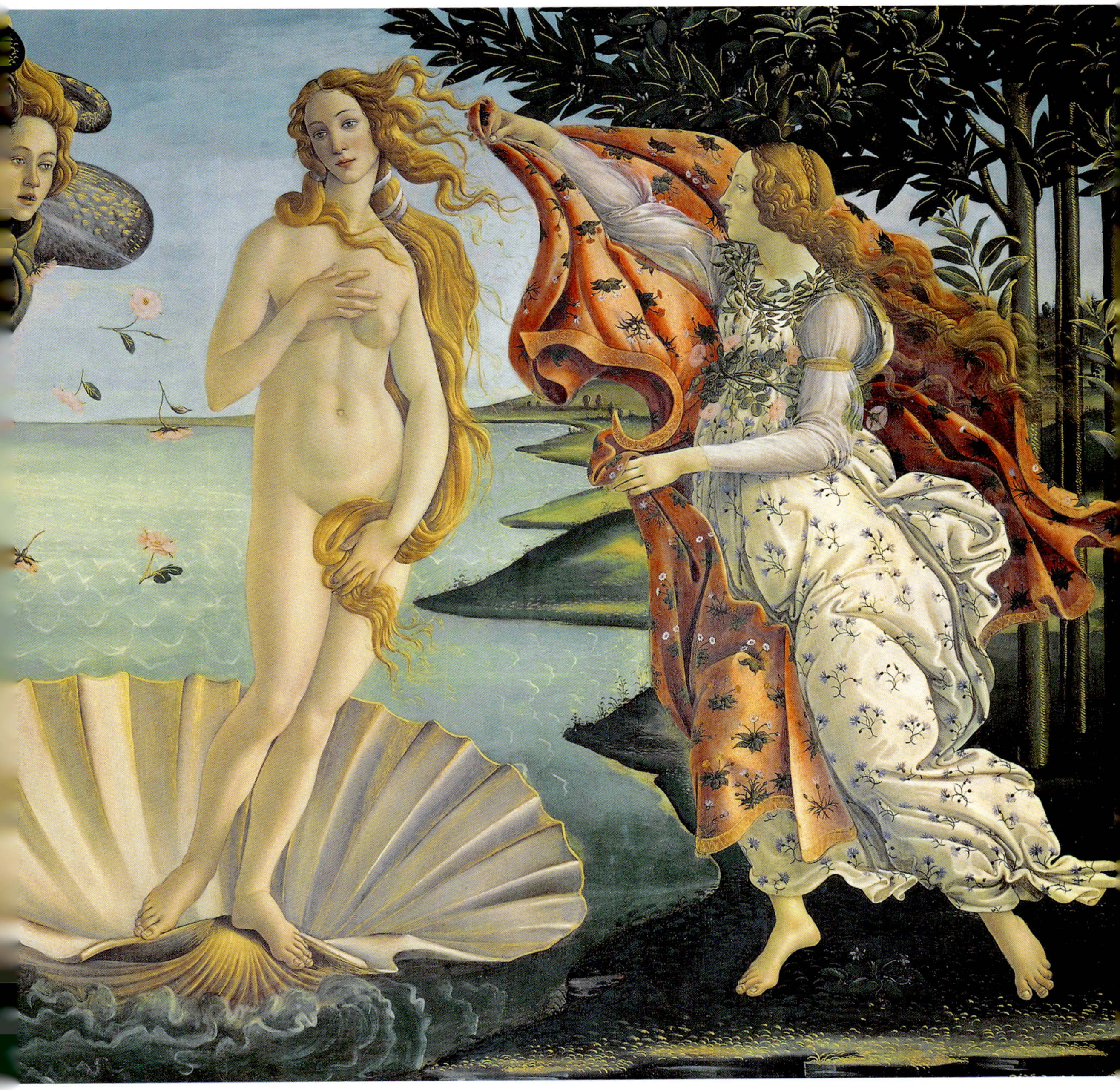

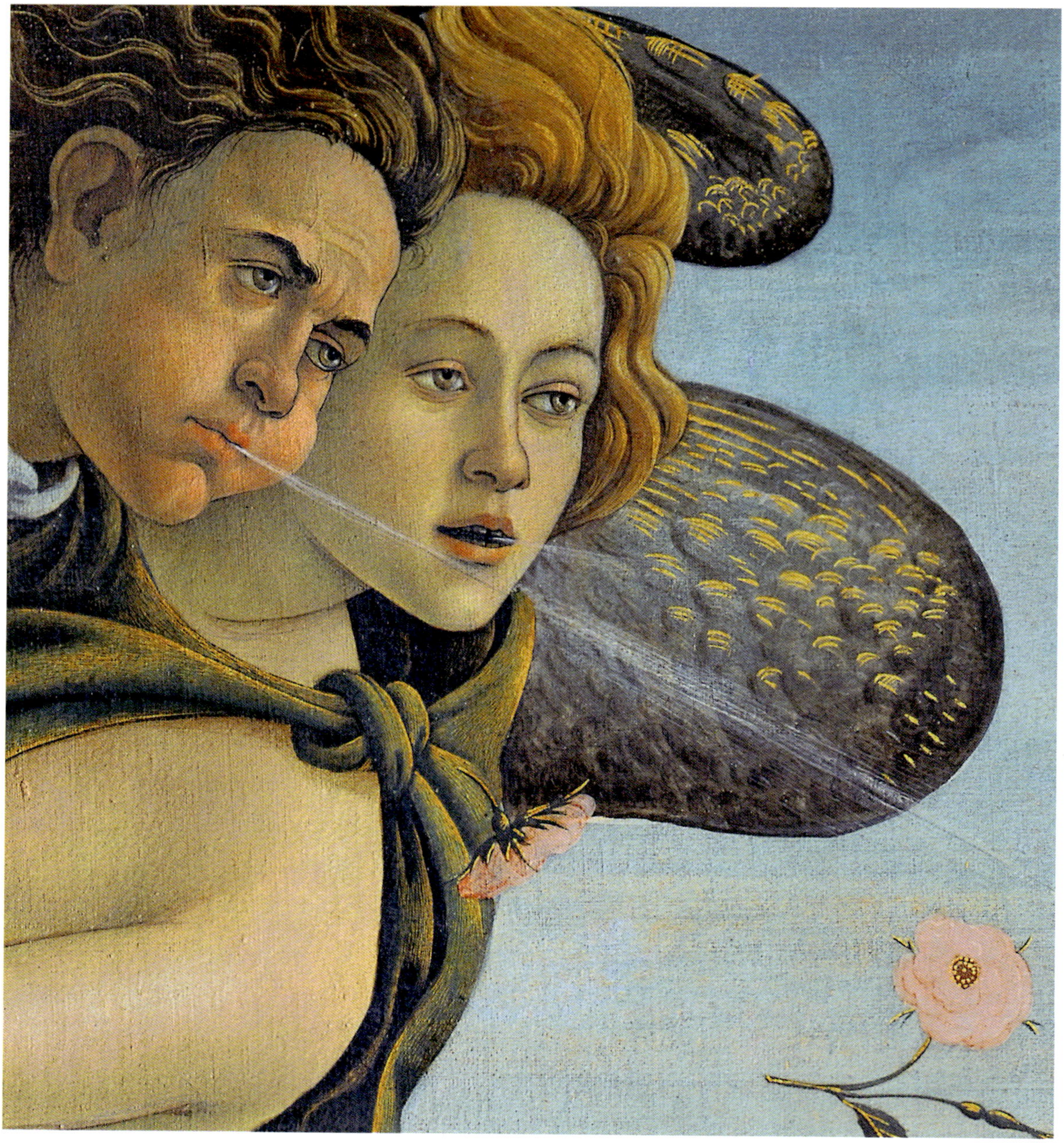

the right side of the hair of Venus, which is flame coloured) and from the union of the spirit with the theme. As with the *Calumny* of the younger Apelles (see p. 40), the painting has a classic precedent in the *Venus Anadyomene* of the elder Appelles (IV century A.D.). Cited by various ancient sources, this work – of which we have a more precise idea today, thanks to a copy from Pompei unknown at the time of Botticelli – is described by the humanist Agnolo Poliziano (*Stanze*, I, 99-103) in such a way as to allude rather more to Sandro's picture than the original model. The technical and stylistic characteristics of the *Birth of Venus* induce us to align the dating with *Pallas and the Centaur*, placing it after Sandro's stay in Rome. Confirming the close relationship between the sponsor and the location for the paintings – executed for the house in Via Larga – is their actual height, which originally would have been identical: the *Birth of Venus* differs only because, as we can conclude from the composition (the wing of Zephyrus is cut short), the canvas must have been "trimmed" – maybe due to some later damage – by around 35 centimetres.

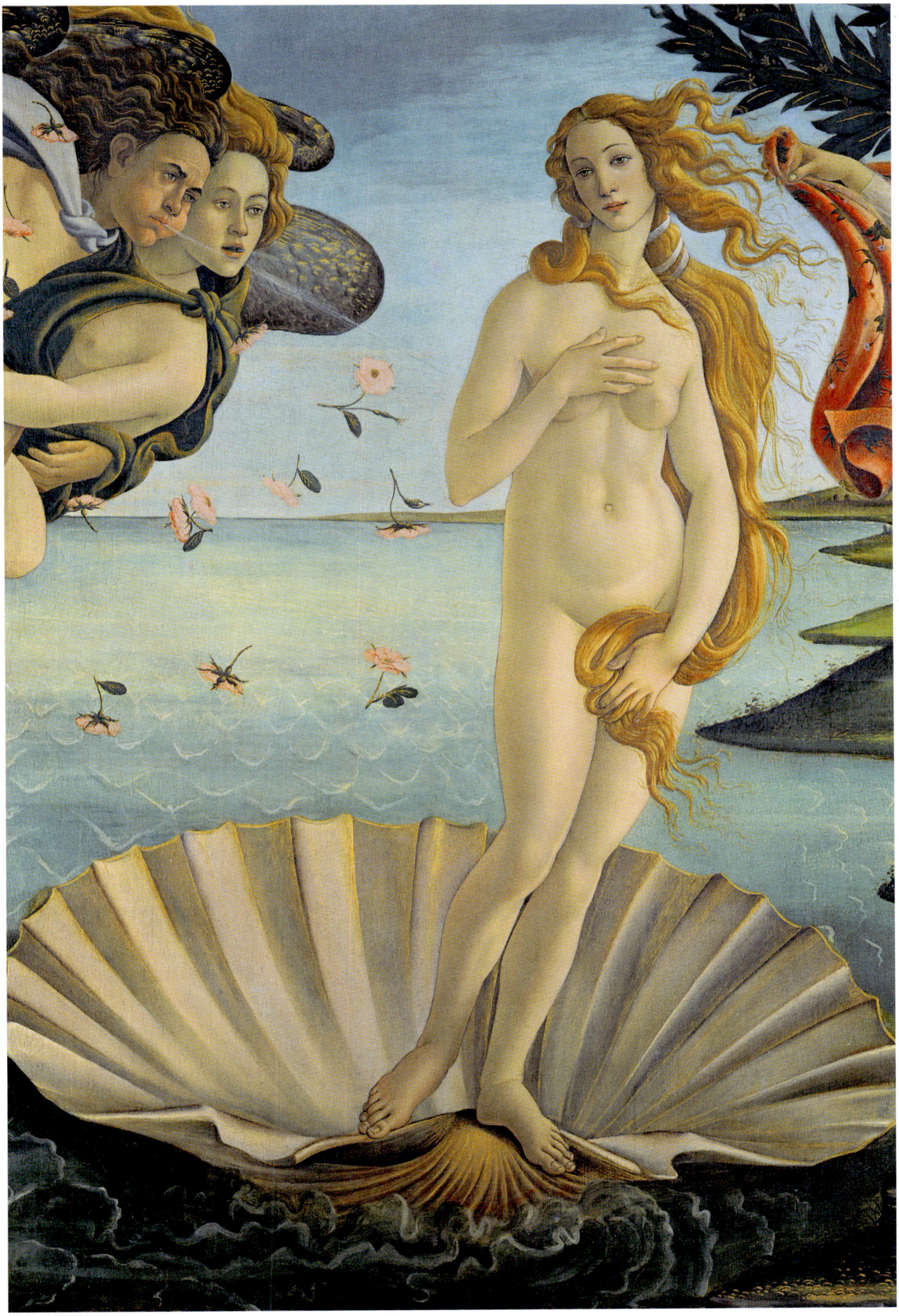

MADONNA AND CHILD ENTHRONED BETWEEN FOUR ANGELS AND SIX SAINTS (ST. BARNABAS ALTARPIECE)
1487, tempera on panel, 268 x 280 cm

On June 11, 1289, the Florentines defeated the militia of Arezzo on the plain of Campaldino. Special honours were bestowed on saints whose feast days fell on a victorious date, and being June 11 and the feast of St. Barnabas, the victors decided to dedicate a church to him (1322). The patronage for this building fell to the Medici and Speziali clans, and in the last decade of the fifteenth century its consuls commissioned Botticelli to paint a large panel for the main altar. The painting remained in its original location until 1700, when it was transferred to the back wall. In 1717 the painter and restorer Agostino Veracini added the arch and the canopy over the two roundels behind the throne; in these circumstances, the dais that served as the base for the principal painting was removed. In 1808, a Napoleonic decree sanctioned the "suppression" (i.e. the confiscation by the State) of the church and the annexed convent: the altarpiece went to the Academy, where it remained until 1919, when it passed the Uffizi. At this point, Veracini's additions were eliminated and the four surviving elements of the original seven on the dais were put back in (not reproduced here).
At the centre of the composition is the Virgin and Child in a gesture of blessing, seated on a throne featuring classic lines and the "choicest forms"(Argan); at head height are two pairs of angels facing each other, two of which hold up the drapes of the canopy while the other two show the symbols of the Passion, respectively, the crown and nails of the cross. In the foreground, at the bottom, are six saints: from left, Catherine of Alexandria, Augustine and Barnabas; right, John the Baptist, Ignatius and the Archangel Michael. At the back, on either side of the throne, but higher up, two monochrome roundels with a gold background depict the annunciating Archangel Gabriel (left) and the annunciated Madonna (right). On the base of the throne we can read, on three lines, the verse VIRGIN MOTHER / DAUGHTER OF YOUR / SON, with which Dante begins the prayer of Bernard of Clairvaux (Paradise, XXXIII, 1).
It should be noted that, in integrating the painting with the completion of the upper arch of which the top of the canopy was a part, Veracini necessarily had to change some essential elements, removing them from the original. Despite having lost something in terms of balance and consistency of composition, the work remains remarkable: behind the classic measurements of the architecture and the composure of the characters, we can perceive an intense pathos and a deep religiosity.

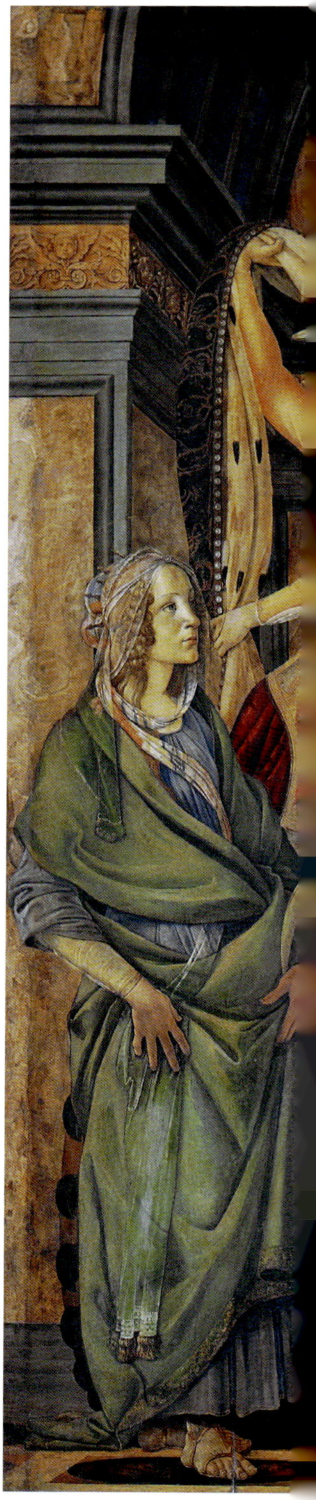

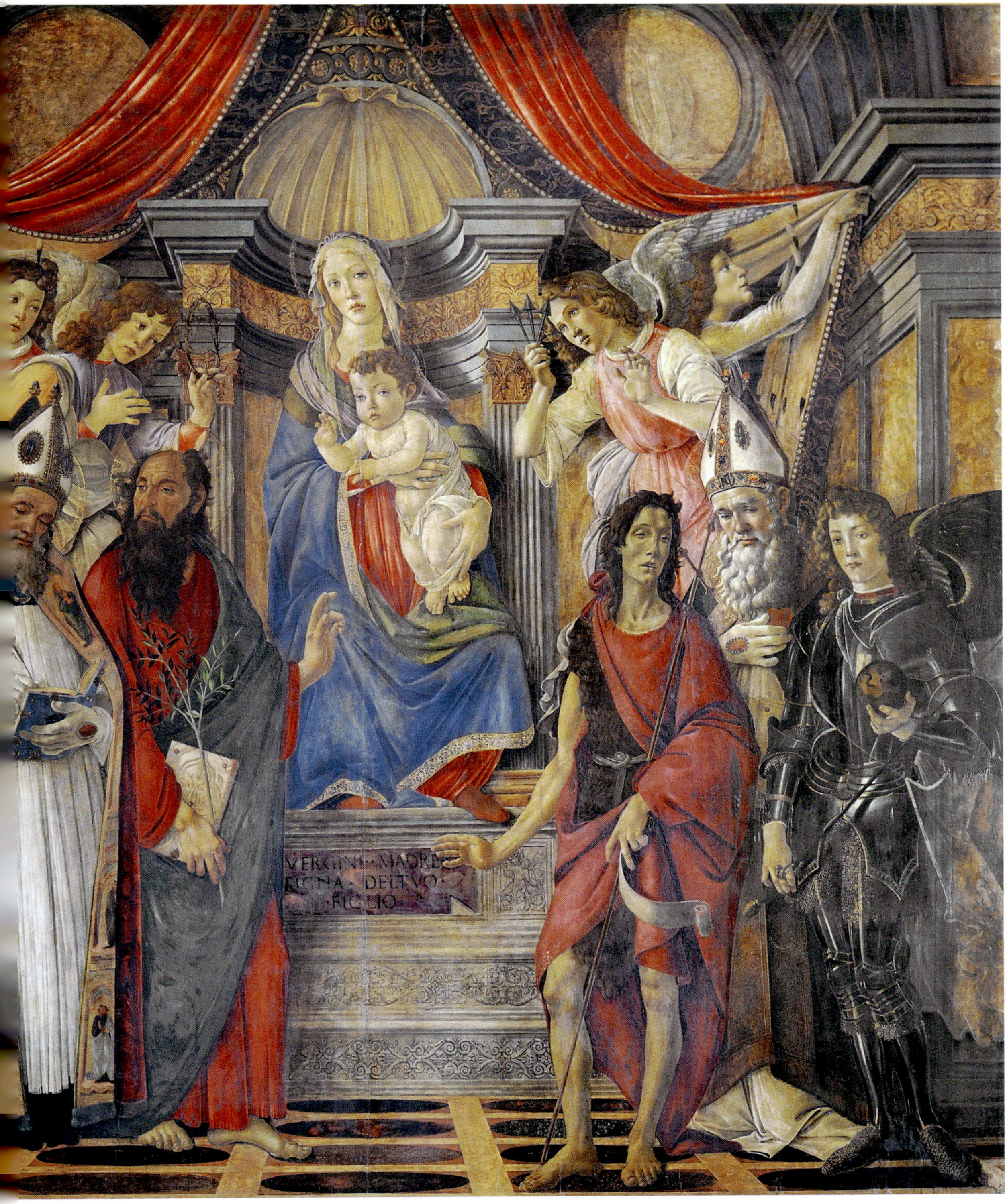
VERGINE·MADRE
DEL TVO·
·FIGLIO·

MADONNA OF THE POMEGRANATE
c. 1487, tempera on panel, ∅ 143.5 cm

This *tondo* was in the collection of Cardinal Leopoldo de 'Medici; on his death (1675) it passed into the collections of the Grand Dukes of Tuscany. Its definitive transfer to the Uffizi took place in 1780.
Starting from an analysis of its beautiful carved and gilded frame – perhaps from the workshop of Giuliano da Sangallo – in 1908 Herbert Horne identified this *Madonna* as the *tondo* that Botticelli was commissioned to paint by the magistrates of the Massai di Camera for their audience chamber in the Palazzo Vecchio (1487) . In fact, the golden lilies on a blue field forming the decoration of the frame are not the Florentine lily, but the *fleurs de lys* of the crown of France, which some twenty years before, courtesy of Louis XI, had joined the Medici coat of arms. Now, the very presence of this symbol shows that the work was intended for a public use.
Surrounded by six angels praying, this Virgin displays traits of extraordinary nobility and sadness, her head slightly tilted to the right and her eyes lost in a remote distance, holding the Child in her arms. Both hold the pomegranate in their left hands, whose cut reveals the blood coloured seeds, foretelling the Passion of Christ. The wreaths of roses carried by the two angels in the foreground are a clear allusion to the Rosary, the prayer that in those years took the form it still has today and whose initial formula, "HAIL [MARY] FULL OF GRACE (gratia)" is embroidered on the robe of the left-hand angel.
Compared to the previous *Madonna of the Magnificat*, the difficulties associated with the art of composition for a round work of art are resolved by arranging the angels symmetrically. The refined use of colour and the conscious use of symbolism (as well as roses there are lilies, the symbol of virginal purity) confirm that Sandro has reached full artistic maturity.

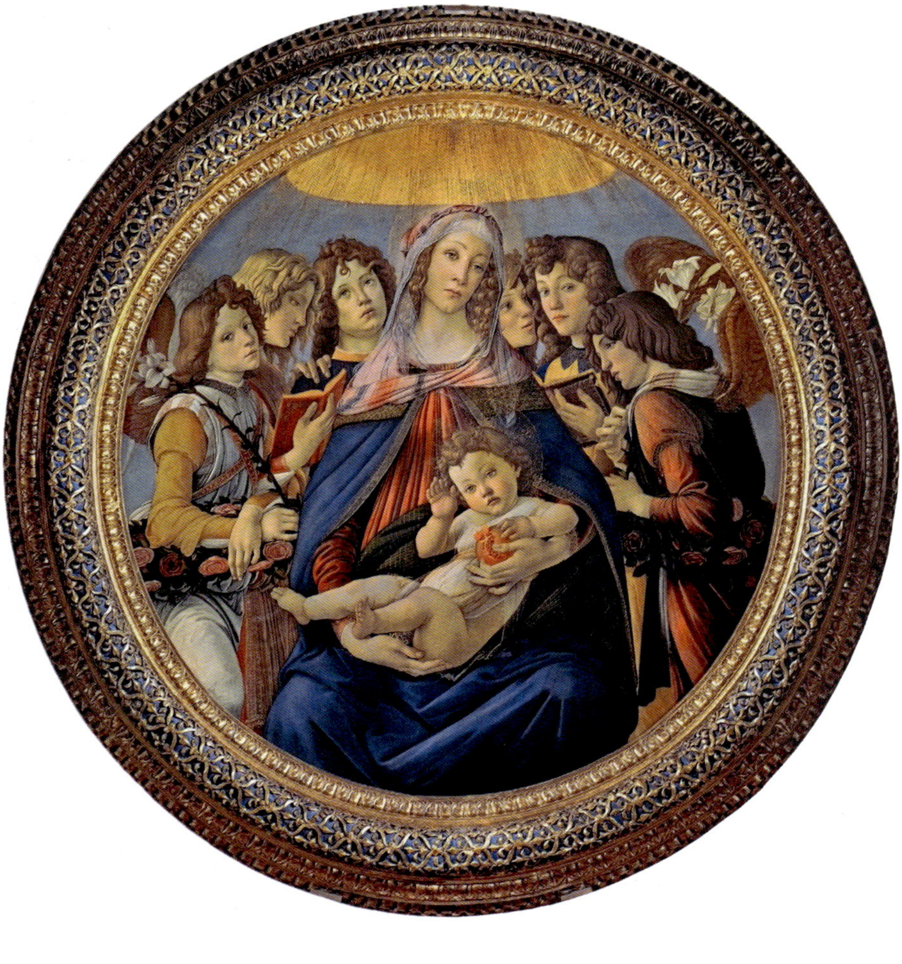

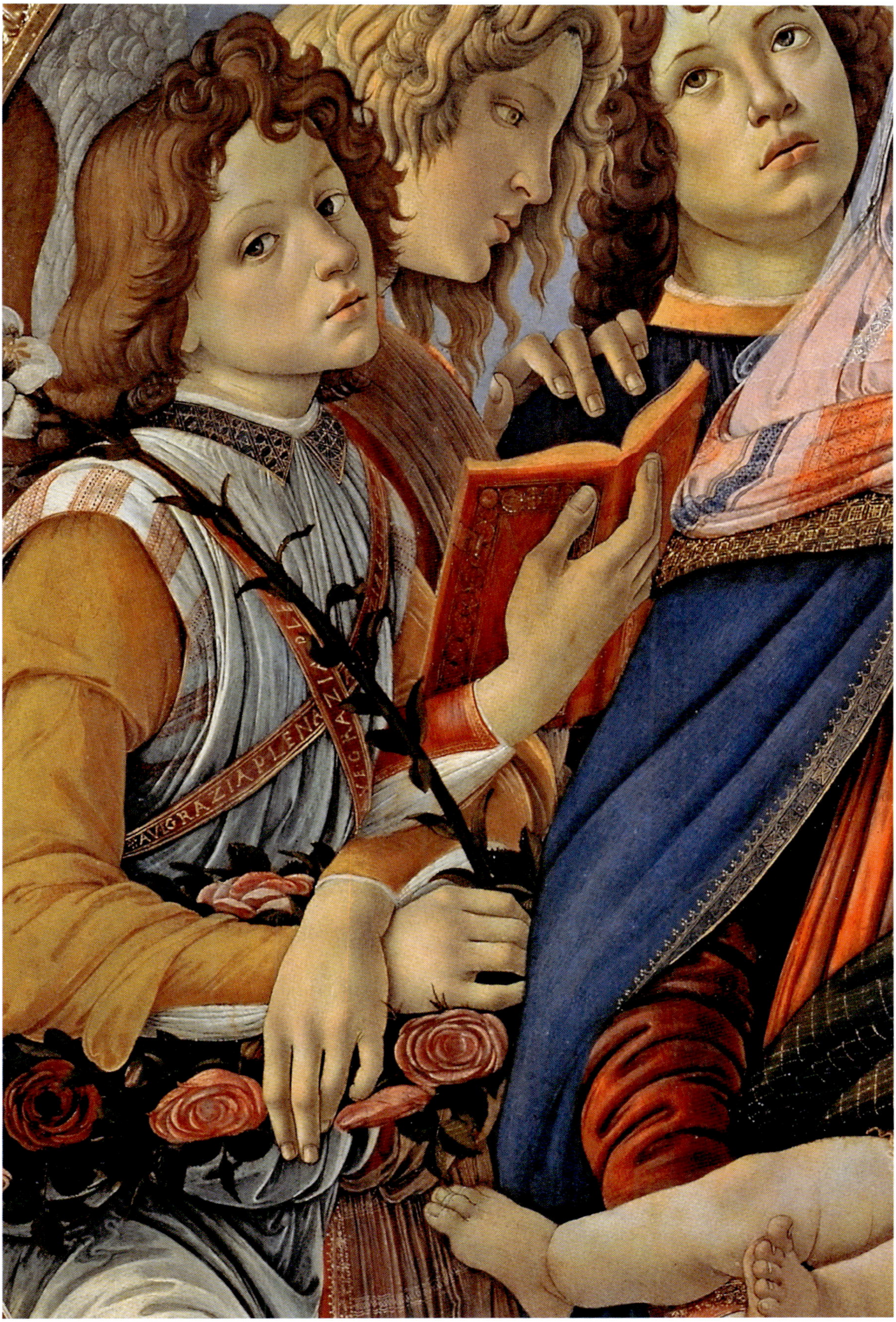

THE CESTELLO ANNUNCIATION
1489, tempera on panel, 150 x 156 cm

This work has survived in its original, architectural-style frame, which carries on the bottom the classic evangelical greeting – arranged in two blocks divided by a small *Pietà* of Christ which, by the nature of its quality, can be assigned to Sandro's workshop – along with the two coats of arms of the work's patron.

We know plenty about the history of this painting. The book of the benefactors of the Cestello monastery in Borgo Pinti (and not the self-named complex in Oltrarno) precisely records the commission, entrusted to Botticelli in May 1489. A banker, Benedetto di Ser Francesco Guardi del Cane ordered the panel, paying Sandro thirty ducats for the work.

The *Annunciation* served to decorate the family chapel in the church of Cestello, newly renovated by the architect Giuliano da Sangallo. In 1669 the church and convent were rededicated to the Florentine mystic St. Mary Magdalene de 'Pazzi; the altarpiece, however, remained in its place until the second half of the eighteenth century. Moved to the small chapel of the Villa of San Martino in Terenzano at Fiesole, belonging to the monks of the order, the painting was rediscovered in 1870 and two years later was transferred to the Uffizi.

The interior shown is typical of a noble Florentine house of the period, with a terracotta floor divided in squares by strips of white marble, which confer profound perspective on the work. At the back, on the left, a door with a moulded cornice of stone leads us beyond a small garden surrounded by a white wall to a clear view of Flemish inspiration, crossed by a meandering river.

On the far left there is another door, essential for the simplicity of the composition as it provides a second source of light for the scene, creating the soft luminosity that characterises the art of Sandro. It is precisely through this door that the angel enters, or rather swoops in, kneeling and curbing his flight all in one movement. His energy is counterbalanced by the surprise and dismay of the Virgin, who flexes in the opposite direction. In the natural need for balance, her right arm reaches out toward the raised arm of the angel, creating the first diagonal; another inverted line runs from the lily in the angel's hand and through the left hand side of the landscape.

This is a masterpiece of harmonious composition, obtained via the simplest means and devoid of any decorative excesses.

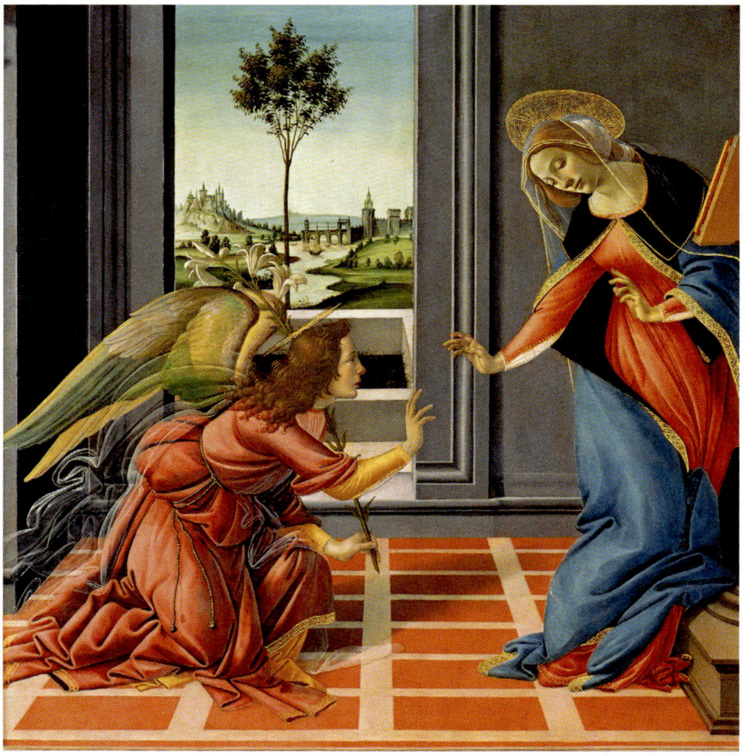

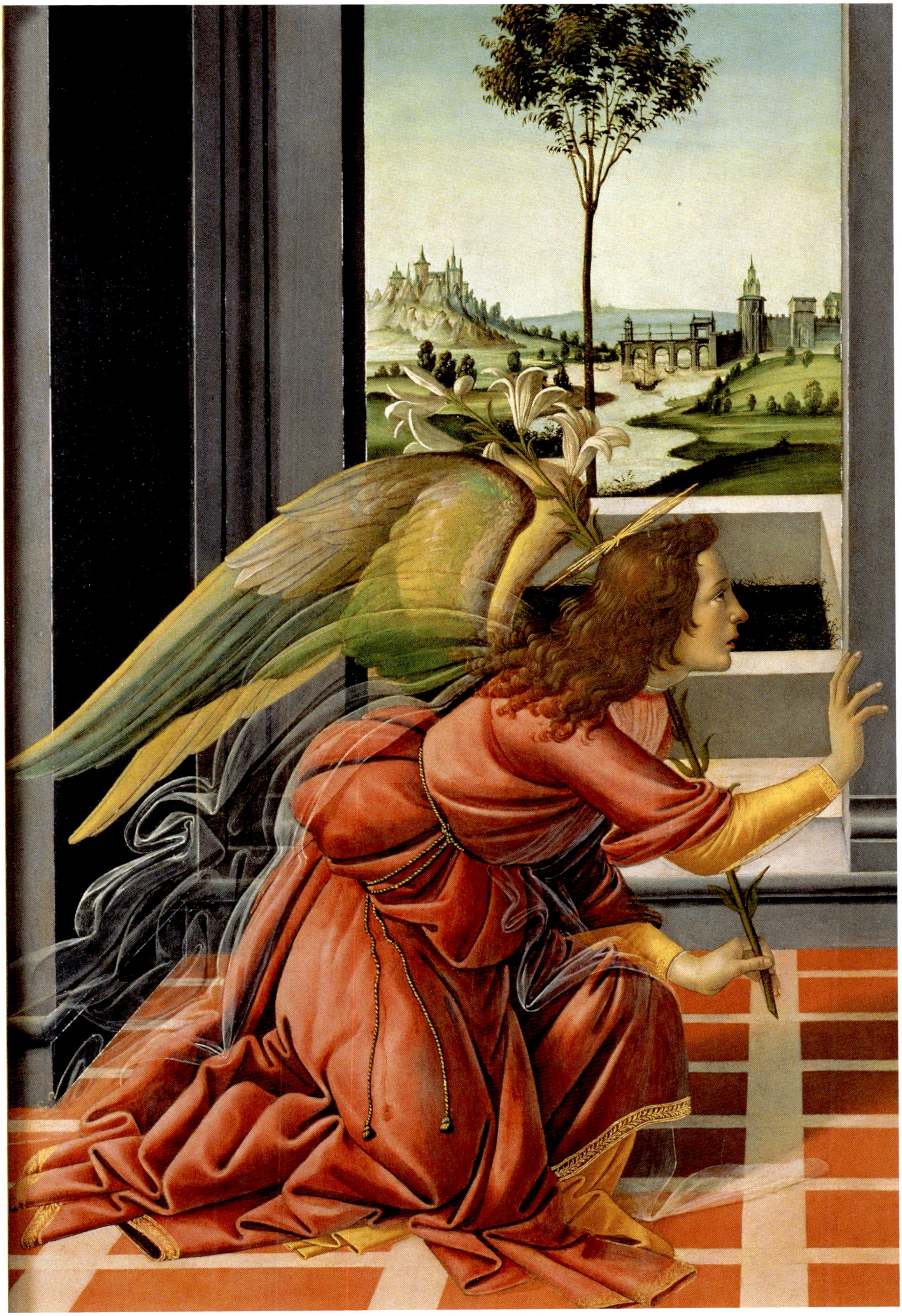

SAINT MARK ALTARPIECE

Saint Eligius (known in Italy as Eligio or Alò) lived in France between the sixth and seventh century, and was bishop of Noyon. Before taking his vows, however, he was famed as a goldsmith, plying his trade with such legendary honesty that the king of France, Clotaire II and his successor, Dagobert I, made him grand treasurer of the kingdom. Hence his later election as the patron saint of goldsmiths.
In the church of St. Mark, the Guild of Silk Weavers, which also included goldsmiths, were responsible for the care of Saint Eligius' chapel. In the 1580s this company took on the work of restructuring the chapel; as it approached completion, they commissioned a large altarpiece from Botticelli. In 1596, in connection with the changing taste of the time, the work was replaced with a *Transfiguration* by Giovan Battista Paggi (1554-1627) and was moved into the Chapter of the adjoining convent. In 1807, with the Napoleonic "suppression" which we have already mentioned in connection with the altarpiece of St Barnabas (see p. 28), the painting was moved to the Academy and in 1919, to the Uffizi. Its poor condition made it difficult to appreciate its qualities, leading even to the speculation that Sandro's pupil Filippino Lippi had had a hand in it alongside his master. Only the long and detailed restoration which was completed in 1990 underlined its great value; today, the Saint Mark altarpiece is considered one of the key works of Botticelli's artistic maturity, also in the light of the panel's innovative division in two main areas.

THE CORONATION OF THE MADONNA AND FOUR SAINTS
1489-90, tempera on panel, 378 x 258 cm

In the foreground, at the bottom – against a very spare landscape in terms of the economy of its composition – are four saints: from left to right, John the Evangelist, Augustine, Jerome and Eligius. The first three are depicted holding books, because in their works celestial events are mentioned, which manifest themselves in the upper part of the painting. At the top, against a background featuring a sunburst of gold, is the Virgin crowned by God the Father; as in the later *Mystic Nativity*, the scene is surrounded by a choir of angels. Despite their classical composure, all the figures portrayed in the altarpiece resonate with vibrant expressiveness that already heralds the final "Savonarola" phase of Sandro's artistic history.
The dais (not reproduced here) consists of a single tablet 21 cm high and 269 cm long. The five sacred *Histories*, divided by painted columns, represent: 1) *St. John the Evangelist on Patmos*, where the saint, exiled to the Greek island by the emperor Domitian, writes his visions of the *Revelation* on the seashore; 2) *St. Augustine in his Cell*, in a version defined by dramatic *chiaroscuro*; 3) the *Annunciation*, 4) *St. Jerome Penitent*, 5) *History of St. Eligius*. According to tradition, Eligius also worked as a blacksmith in his youth. Here the saint, having to shoe a possessed horse, cuts off one of its front legs: after having applied the horseshoe, he reattaches the leg with a sign of the cross. At the centre of the image, between the horse and the saint, a horned woman hides her mutilated nose. The image alludes to another legend according to which Satan, in feminine clothes, had once tried to enter Eligius' forge; recognising the devil, he had cut off his nose with red-hot pincers. Both stories are inspired by Scandinavian folklore and not, as was once though, the *Golden Legend* of Jacopo da Voragine.

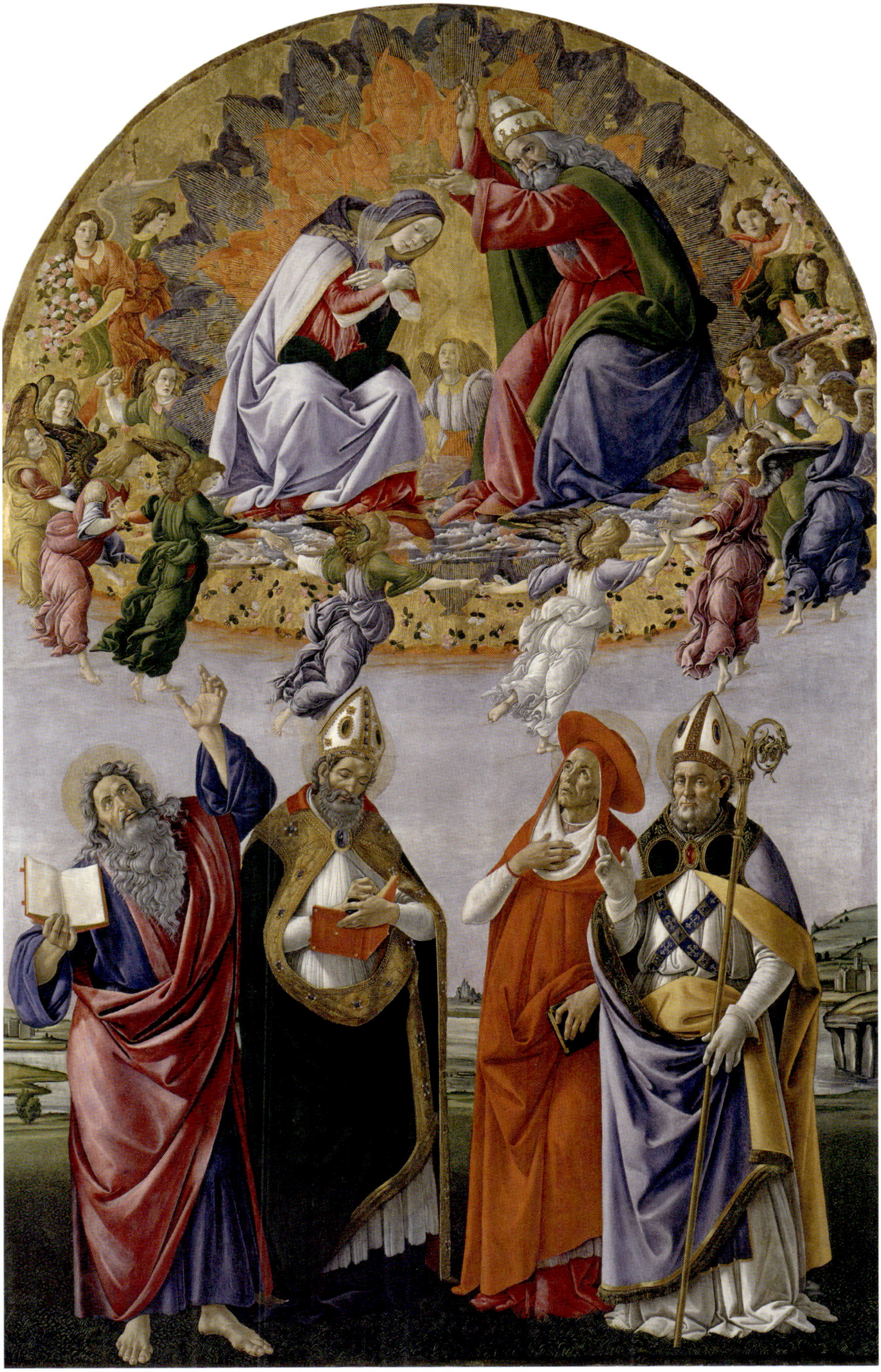

ST. AUGUSTINE IN HIS CELL

1490-1494, tempera on panel, 41 x 27 cm

This panel was part of Bernardo Vecchietti's collection of paintings, where it was seen by Vasari, who refers to Filippo Lippi in the second edition of the *Lives*. Fifteen years later, however, the Florentine playwright and art critic Raffaello Borghini, in his dialogue *Il Riposo* (1584), refers to "a beautifully painted picture" by Botticelli, with no mention of Filippo as one of the artists in Vecchietti's collection. In 1771, the painting passed to the painter and collector Ignazio Hugford (1703-1778), upon whose death it went to the engraver Pieralli Piero, who in 1779 gave it to the Uffizi Gallery. Thrown off the scent by Vasari, scholars continued to endorse the work's attribution to Filippo until 1877, when the scholar Giovanni Morelli suggested the name of Sandro, which found consensus amongst later critics.

Indeed Botticelli's hand is apparent in every element of this example of virtuosity of "minute detail". This is a work of devotion for private use, made for a connoisseur, a masterpiece to be carefully examined. The saint is shown from the front, sitting at his desk. As in the Ognissanti *St. Augustine*, he wears bishop's robes; the black scapular rather indicates his role as founder of the order which bears his name. He writes; the nervous posture of his hands (the execution of which is reminiscent of *Calumny*, allowing us to make an initial approximate chronological hypothesis) along with the broken quills and crumpled sheets scattered on the ground seem to allude to a powerful source of inspiration with which he can barely keep up. The light that comes from the left is softened by a thin curtain, little more than a veil, whose movement emphasises the motion of the saint's head and body.

The interior, which exudes exquisite Renaissance taste – recalling Giuliano da Sangallo's contemporary sacristy for Santo Spirito – is a cell with a beamed and wood-lined ceiling; the lighting effects conferred upon the stone are exceptional. At the back of the cell, in the half moon created by the curve of the ceiling is a Madonna and Child, a monochromatic oval of masterful workmanship. Monochrome medallions are also hung on the arches of the spandrels; the two profiles are possibly the emperors Arcadius and Honorius, who at the time of Augustine (between the fourth and fifth centuries) ruled over a Roman empire definitively divided in two.

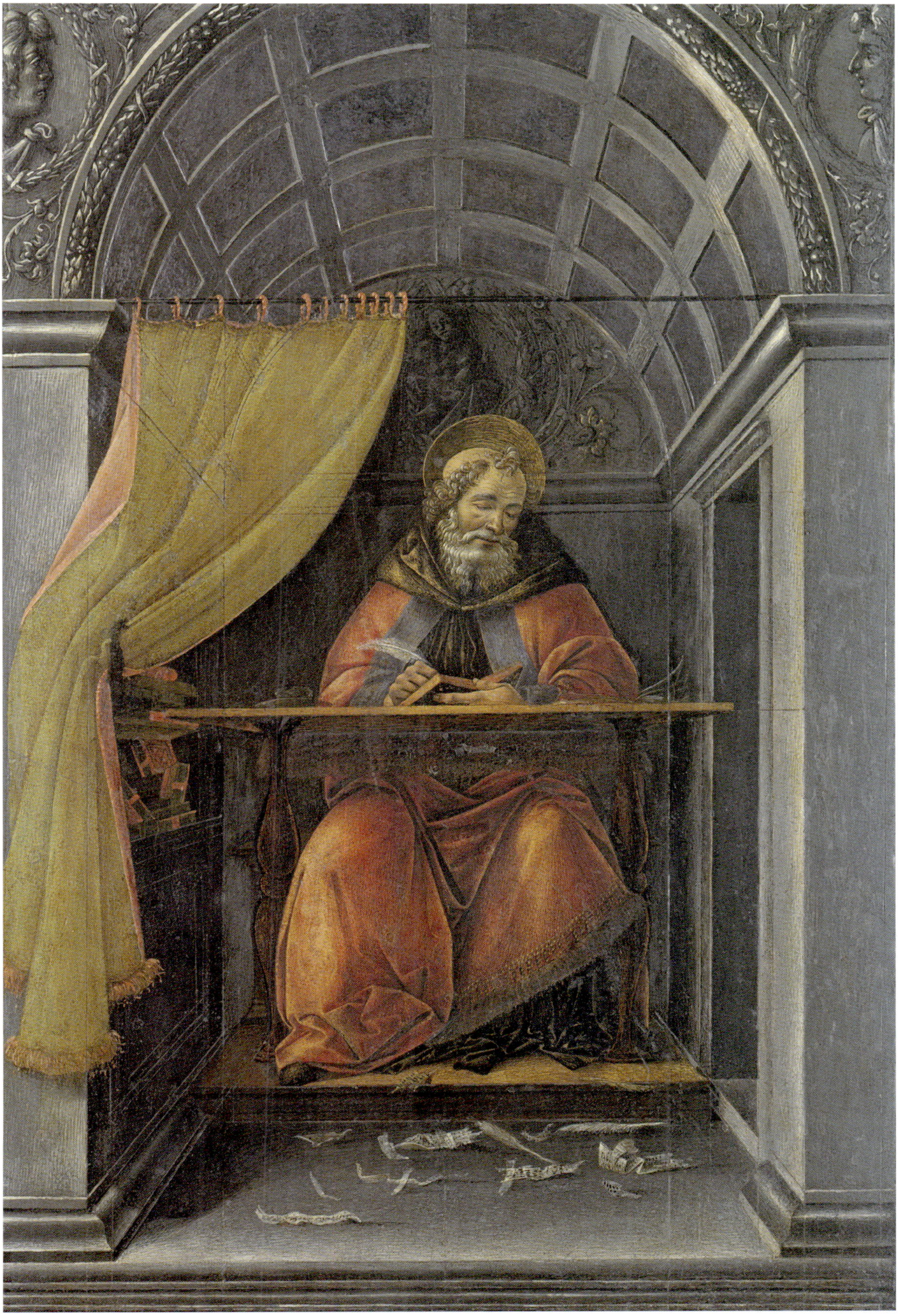

CALUMNY OF APELLES
c. 1497, tempera on panel, 62 x 91 cm

Giorgio Vasari speaks of this panel in the first edition of the *Lives* (1550), claiming to have seen it in the house of the Segni family. In fact, it had been donated by the painter to Antonio Segni, his close friend; and his son Fabio, who inherited it on Antonio's death, affixed two Latin couplets to the frame:

INDICIO QUEMQUAM NE FALSO LAEDERE TENTENT
TERRARUM REGES PARVA TABELLA MONET
HUIC SIMILEM AEGYPTI REGI DONAVIT APELLES
REX FUIT ET DIGNUS MUNERE MUNUS EO,

which translates more or less in the following manner: "This picture is a warning to the kings of the earth against trying to harm anyone on the basis of false evidence. Apelles gave such a picture to the King of the Egyptians. The King was worthy of the gift, as was the gift of the King."
Given that the painting arrived in the Uffizi in 1704 and, after being transferred to the secret Archive of Palazzo Pitti, returned permanently to the Gallery in 1773, it is perhaps logical to question what motivated Botticelli to choose the subject and why he wanted to give to his friend.
It's worth starting from the short essay entitled *Slander*, in which the Greek writer Lucian of Samosata (second century AD) tells an anecdote about the painter Apelles (not the great master of Kos who flourished under Alexander the Great, but a later namesake, born in Colophon and a naturalised Ephesian; even if during the Renaissance the two painters were considered a single person). Apelles, at the court of King Ptolemy Filelfo of Egypt, aroused the jealousy of another artist, a certain Antiphilus, who insinuated to Ptolemy at a banquet that Apelles was the member of a conspiracy. The King, being short on wisdom and the easy victim of flattery, believed the slander and went into a great rage. But Antiphilus' lie was so blatant that Apelles was actually exonerated from accusation by one of the conspirators. It is said then that Ptolemy, seized with remorse, gave the artist a huge sum, and made Antiphilus his slave. To record his close shave, the artist then painted a picture that Lucian describes textually as follows: "On the right sits a man with long ears, like those of Midas: he extends his hand toward Slander, who goes to meet him. There are two women be-

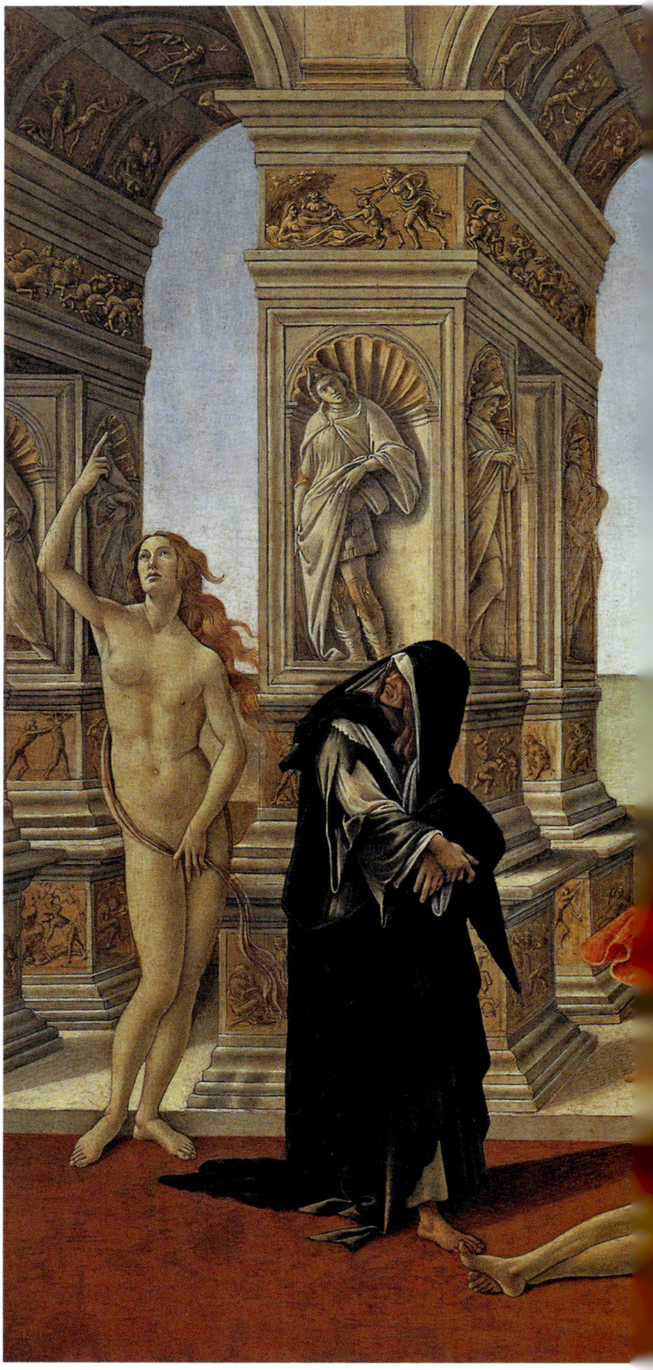

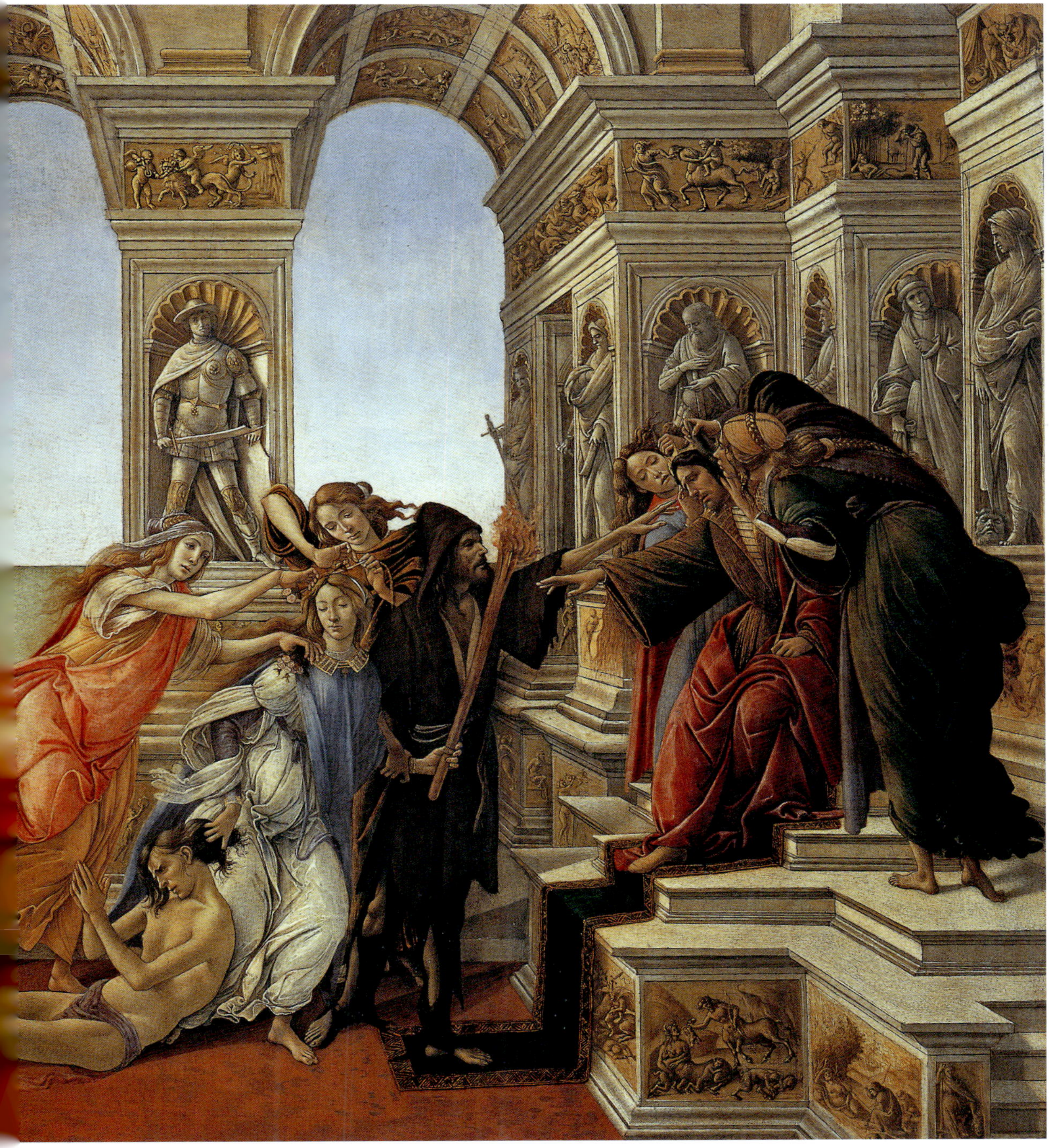

side him, without a doubt Ignorance and Suspicion. On the opposite side, Slander draws near, portrayed as a woman of divine beauty, but with a flushed and agitated face, full of furious rage; she holds in her left a burning torch, while with her right she drags a young man by the hair who, raising his hands to heaven, seems to call the gods to bear witness [to his innocence]. Showing Slander the way is a pale and ugly man with a penetrating gaze who seems drained by a long illness. He is Envy personified. Accusation is accompanied by two other women, who incite her, arrange her clothing and her adornments. The person who explained the allegories in this painting to me said that that one was Malice, and the other Wickedness. Behind them is woman of squalid ap-

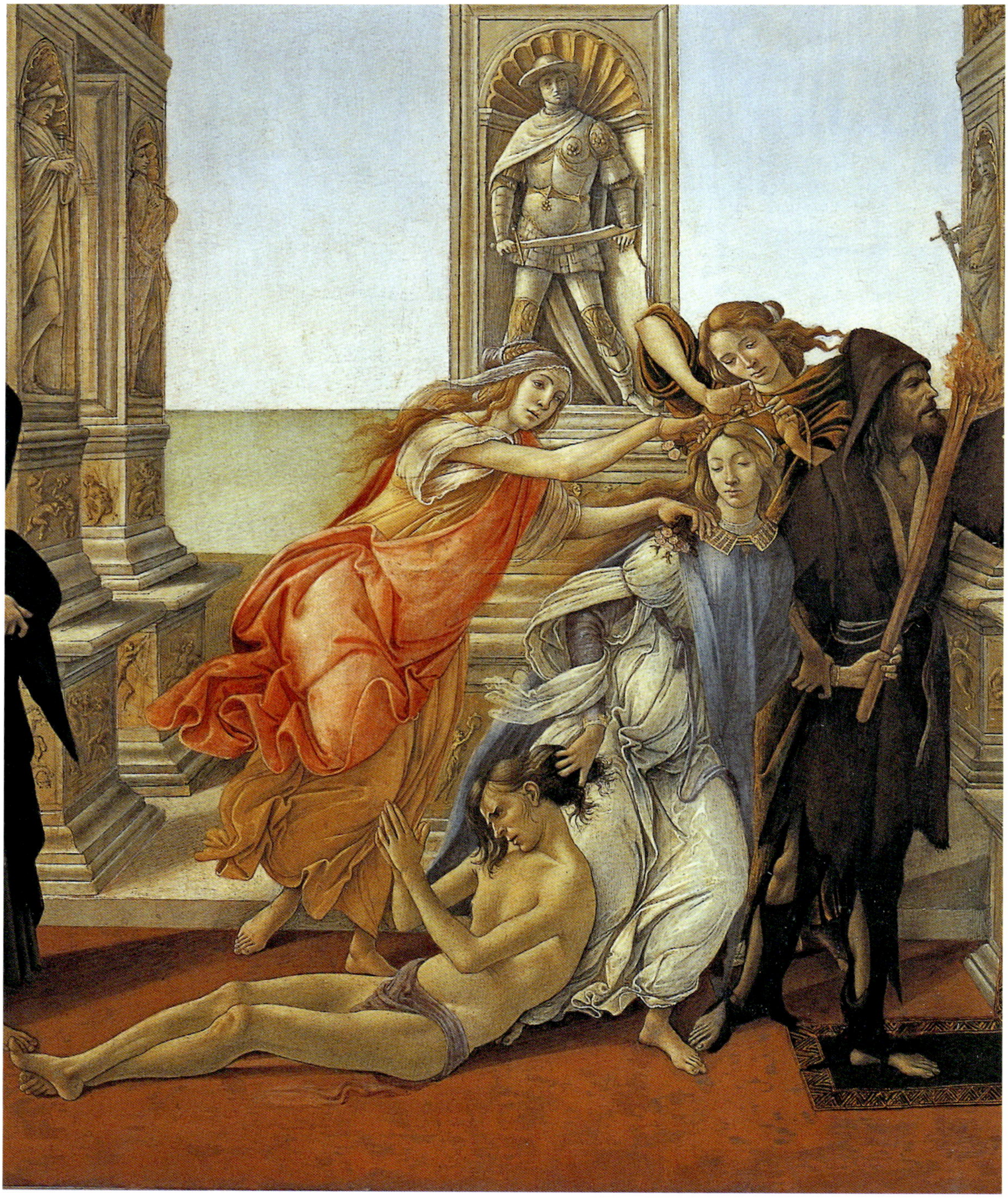

pearance, wearing a black and tattered dress: she is Repentance, who turns her head away, crying and regarding with great dismay the Truth that approaches."

A shorter description of the painting of Apelles – also deriving from Lucian – is found in the *De pictura* of Leon Battista Alberti (1437), but Botticelli's perfect imitation of the scene described by Lucian shows that Sandro must have read *Slander*. The artist would have had easy access to any manuscript: it is perhaps worth noting however that a Latin translation of the works of Lucian came out in Florence in the year 1496. If this was the source, it gives us the earliest possible date for the execution of the painting, which the most recent research suggests took place right around 1497.

Another topic of analysis is the space in which the scene takes place, a throne room along classical lines. At the back, three arches reveal a blue sky over a sea whose pale green hue recalls that of the *Birth of Venus*. The pillars, panelled arches and the right-hand wall of the room – which includes a pedestal for the throne – are adorned with statues and bas-reliefs in gold.

Amongst the subjects depicted are also scenes and characters which are rather alien to classical antiquity (in particular, three episodes from Nastagio degli Onesti's tale, and three references to the stories of Judith), which might seem incomprehensible unless one recognises some of the themes covered by Botticelli in his other paintings. It has been concluded from this that in *Slander* Sandro wanted to allude to a very personal incident, but this hypothesis should be taken with a pinch of salt. One objection among many asks how Botticelli could have resisted the temptation, in that case, to give the victim at least a semblance of his youthful appearance?

But the two alternative theories are not entirely convincing either. According to the first, the victim of slander could have been his friend Segni, for whom the work was destined; but it seems strange that either Segni or his son would not have mentioned it at some point over the years. The second hypothesis suggests that Sandro, in his growing admiration for Savonarola, may have wished to allude to his excommunication (in 1497) or to the tragic end of the Dominican of Ferrara (1498); in that case, though, the dating of the work would have to be moved further forward, probably to the start of the 16th century, which would clash with the stylistic analysis of the artist's later phase.

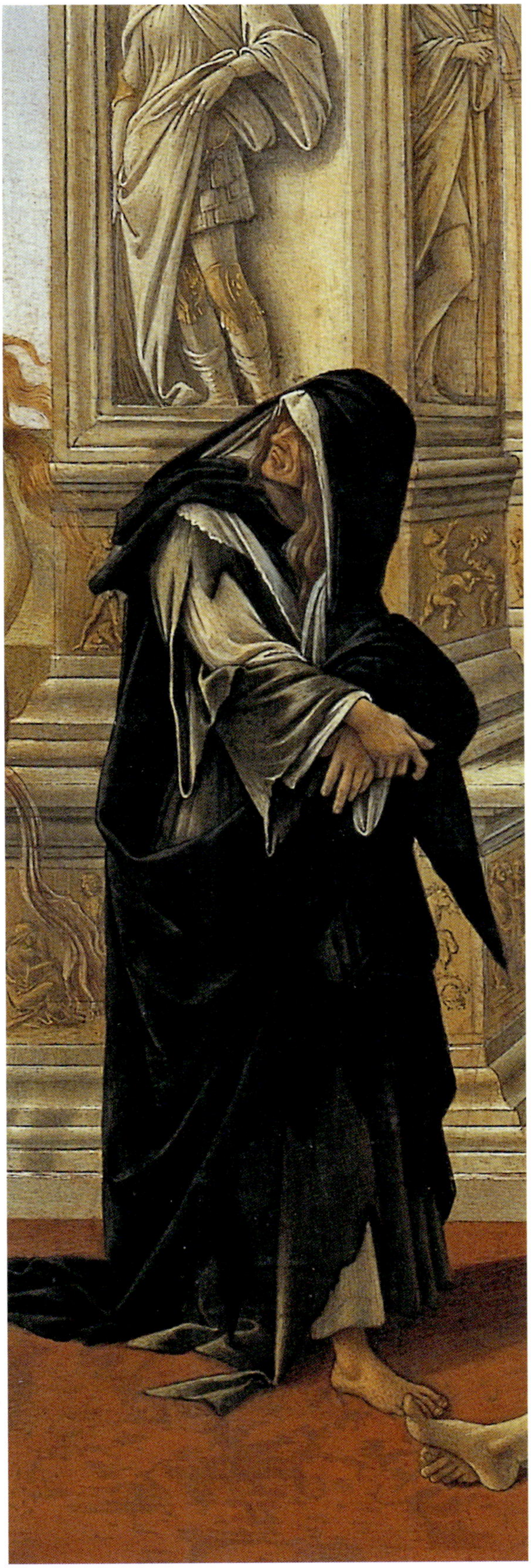

Galleria Palatina, Palazzo Pitti

PORTRAIT OF A YOUNG WOMAN
c. 1485, tempera on panel, 61.3 x 40.5 cm

Simonetta Vespucci, Clarice Orsini, Fioretta Gorini, Lucrezia Tornabuoni, Alfonsina Orsini… the theories about the identity of the maiden shown in this panel are as numerous as they are unsatisfactory, for one reason or another. Scholars do not even agree about Botticelli's authorship of the work: in particular, the sleeve of the garment worn by the girl (a robe with a narrow waist and detached sleeves, called a *camurra*) seems to cover the hand in an inelegant and unnatural way. In opposition to these considerations are those (such as the British historian JW Pope-Hennessy), that focus on the mastery of the two compositional devices: the original asymmetric position of the figure, whose shift towards the left is compensated by the lintel of the door on the right; and the use of dark areas to give more significant emphasis to the profile of the figure. Others have identified some inconsistency in the cut of the dress, concluding that the picture could even be a seventeenth century fake, but the painting, mentioned for the first time in a Palatine Gallery catalogue dating back to 1834, carries a series of clues on its reverse (inventory numbers, affixed tags) from which we can assume that it was in the Medici collections from the seventeenth and eighteenth centuries onwards. It is therefore highly improbable, if not impossible, that the curators of the Gallery would have been fooled by a contemporary sham.

The girl is depicted in profile: this custom, frequently used at the time (if we think of the contemporary feminine portraits by Antonio del Pollaiolo and Ghirlandaio) was designed to enhance the female figure, concealing as much as possible any imperfections. The hair is caught in a "berretta", a sort of cap without laces: a lock of hair hangs from her temple, a detail which gives the picture a jaunty touch of realism which is highly compatible with the young age of the subject. As in the *Portrait of a young woman*, also attributed to Sandro which is kept today in New York, a fine cord is knotted at the girl's throat which disappears into the neck-line of her dress, from which a sacred image presumably hangs. This detail, combined with the complete lack of jewellery, suggests that she is a maiden. We should not forget that by ancient custom the "daughters of the family" in Florence were educated in convents, where they remained almost until the eve of their marriage, naturally arranged by their parents.

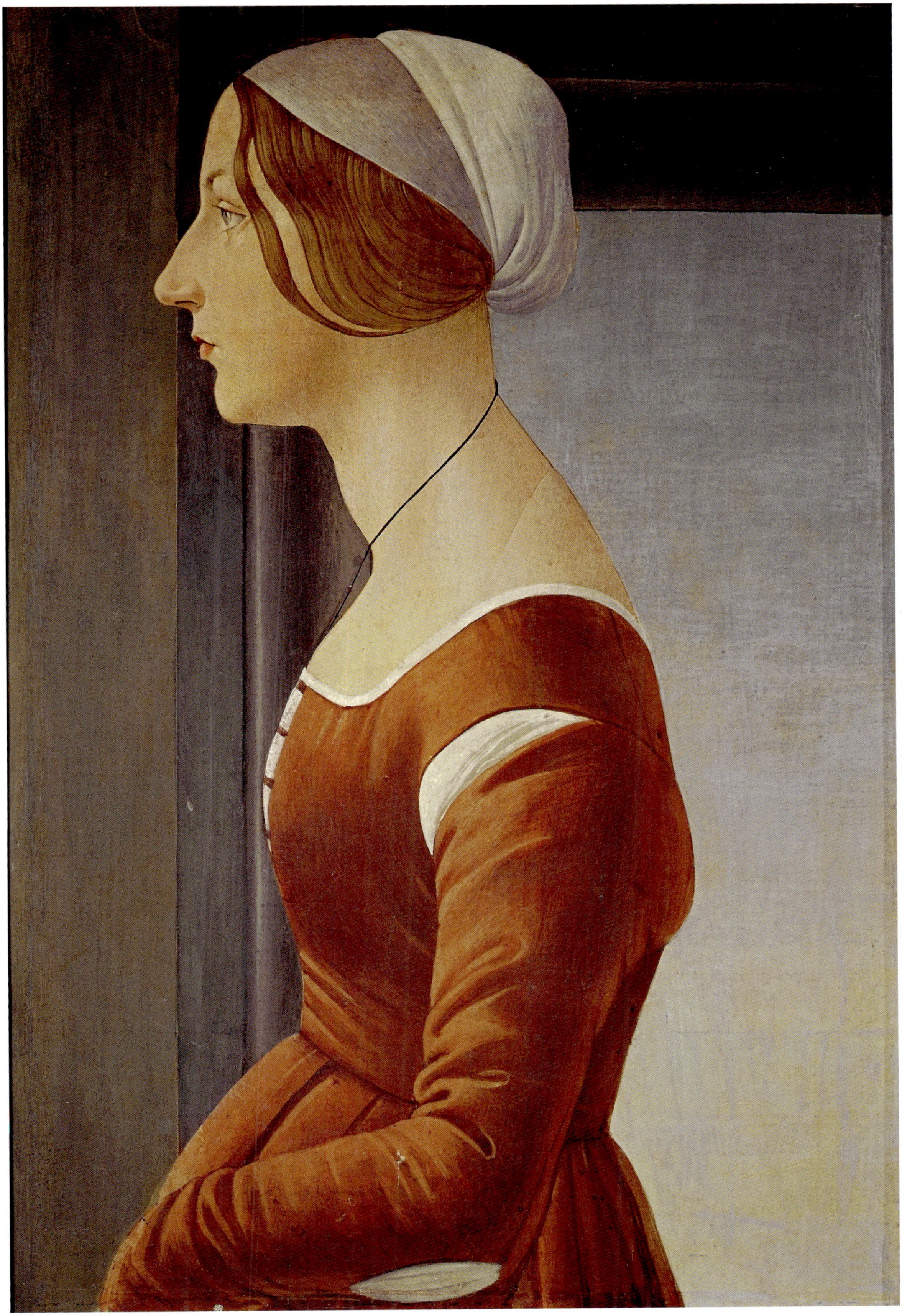

MADONNA WITH CHILD EMBRACED BY THE YOUNG ST. JOHN
c. 1500, tempera on canvas, 134 x 92 cm

This work comes from the Medici-Lorraine collections, implying that it had always belonged to the Medici family. Both the size – too small for an altar of the church – and the subject matter suggest that it was destined for domestic worship. Indirect evidence lies in the fact that there are several other workshop copies, including mirror-image versions, which would have been obtained using the reverse of the sketch: the theme clearly met the public's taste, especially since St. John the Baptist is the patron saint of Florence.
The scene is almost completely occupied by the figures; indeed the usual landscape background is absent. On the left, behind the Virgin, is a flowering rose; on the right, behind St. John, we glimpse a white wall; the sky is blue, an almost leaden shade. The Madonna – extremely elongated as befits Sandro's latter period – bends to carry Jesus into the embrace of his little cousin: and the close position of the two children, surmounted and almost sealed by by the cross that St. John holds in his right hand, symbolically prefigures the Passion of Christ.
The shades of colour, which are rather dark, and the unusually accentuated *chiaroscuro* – note how much light comes directly from one source, bottom right – places the work in the last phase of Sandro's works. The theory dating it to the turn of the sixteenth century seems pretty accurate; its principal proponent, Paul Joannides, identifies shades of the *Madonna and Child with St. John and St. Anne* by Leonardo. In fact, according to Vasari, a preparatory study of da Vinci's famous painting was exhibited for a time in the church of Santissima Annunziata, where it attracted crowds of people. Sandro could not have failed to see it: and we can note how the postures of the Child and Saint John the Baptist in Leonardo's work seem to precede those in the Botticelli painting by a second, almost as if we are looking at two frames in sequence.

Leonardo, *Sketch of Madonna with Child*, detail, National Gallery, London

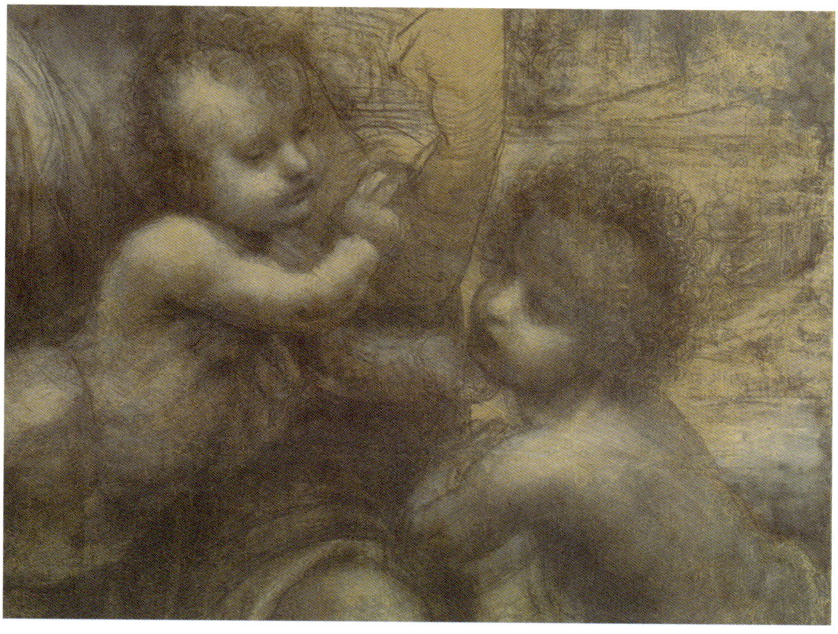

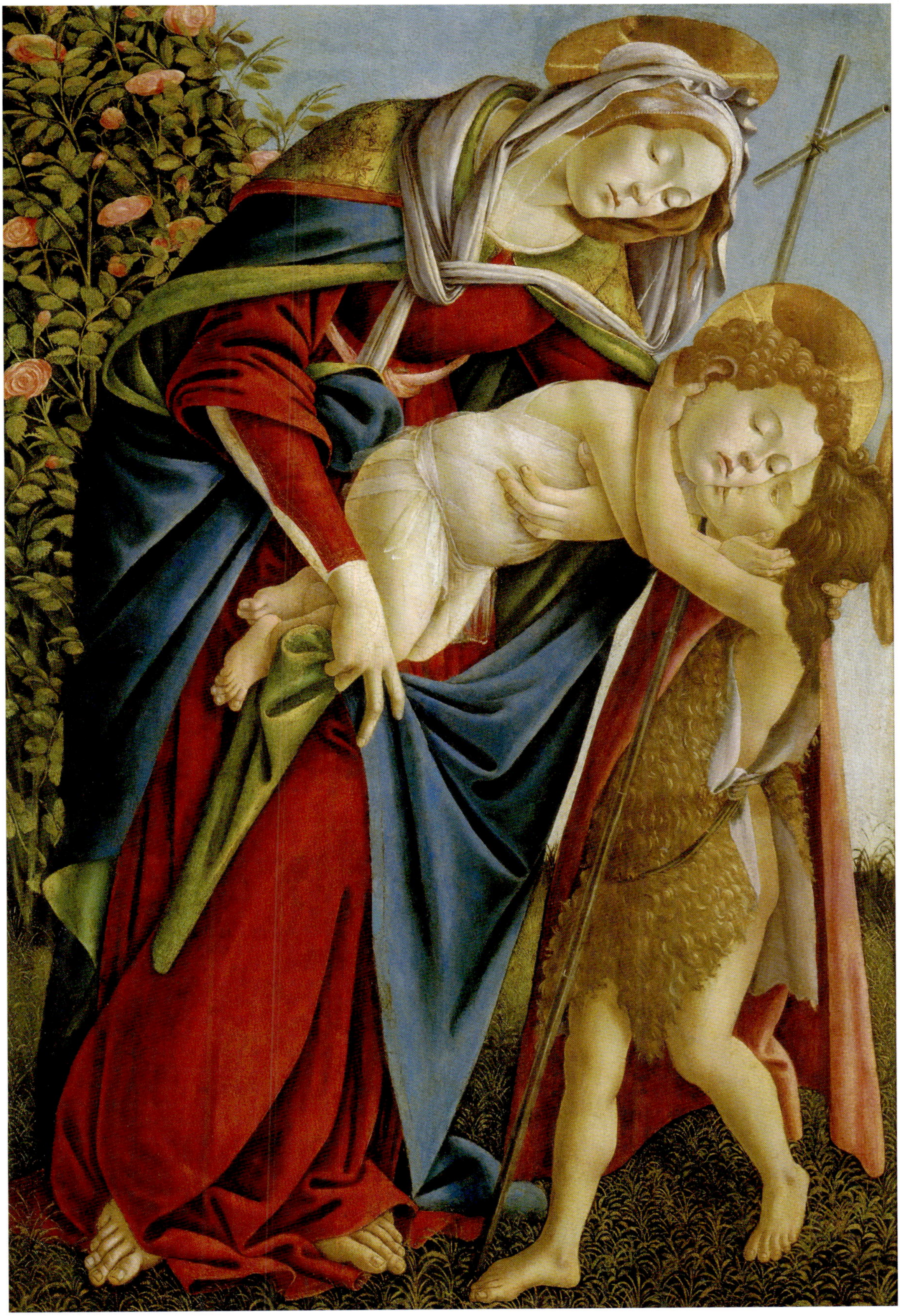

Basilica of Santa Maria Novella

NATIVITY (CRIB)
c. 1476-77, detached fresco, 200 x 300 cm

It is thought that this fresco was originally located in the Lami chapel, for which Sandro painted the famous *Adoration of the Magi* in 1475, now in the Uffizi (see p. 14). At the end of the Lami period of patronage of the chapel, the painting was moved to the opposite wall of the church, to decorate the space above the door. As this took the form of a pointed arch, the fresco, whose original form filled the rounded arch of its primary location, suffered minor adjustments.
The scene does not take place in a wooden stable, but a stone structure. The Child, wrapped in a cloth and leaning against a square stone, holds his arms out towards the kneeling Virgin; on her left, St. John has just arrived, whose presence is highly unusual and indeed uniquely represented here in a Nativity scene. On the opposite side, St. Joseph is sleeping soundly, his bowed head supported by his right hand; in the centre, at the top, the ox and the ass push their muzzles through a large hole in the ruined wall.
For a long time, the fresco was generally attributed to the Florentine school of the fifteenth century; some scholars also cited Filippino Lippi. But in 1932, Berenson identified the hand of Botticelli in the work. This seems particularly plausible for the face of the Virgin and, partially, for St. John; much less so for the figure of the Child. There is an almost an echo of Masaccio or perhaps Masolino in the execution of Saint Joseph. The presence of these additional contributions however does not affect the overall harmony of the painting, which exudes an atmosphere of lively narrative (charming, in particular, are the ox and donkey facing the opening in the wall, which act as fulcrum for the entire composition).

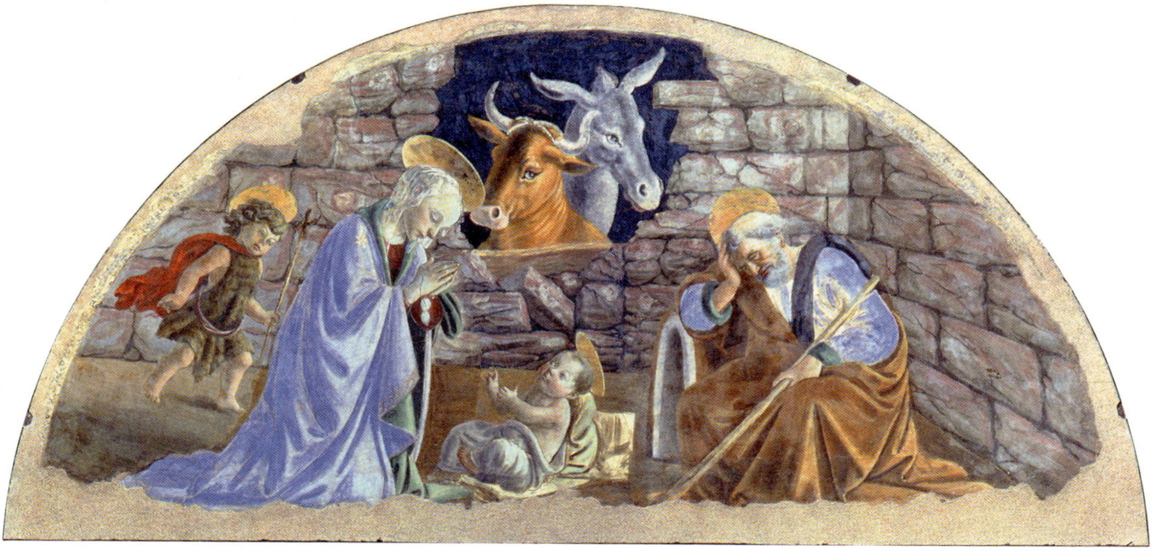

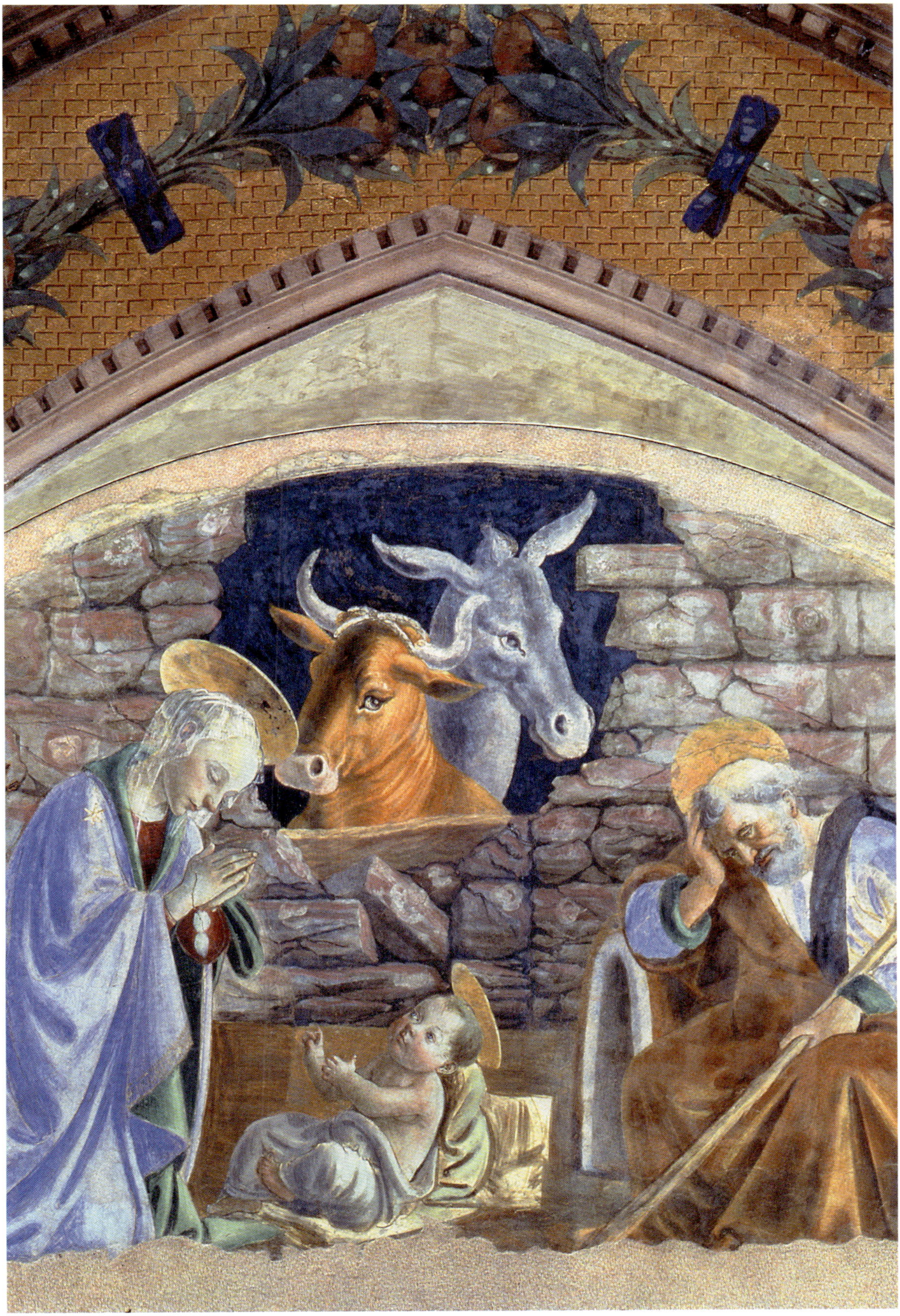

Church of Ognissanti

ST. AUGUSTINE IN HIS CELL
1480, detached fresco, 152 x 112 cm

Before the Council of Trent (1545-1563), the choir was separated from the rest of the nave by a roodscreen, in the centre of which a gate or a door was placed. The roodscreen in the Church of Ognissanti, tall and made of stone, had an altar on the right and another on the left of the door, but between this and any other altar a notable space remained. In 1480, the Umiliati friars decided to decorate the dividing wall with some fake architecture, and use the space between the altars and the door for a painting of the two doctors of the Church: St. Jerome (on the left) and St. Augustine (on the right). The first of the two frescos was allocated to Domenico del Ghirlandaio, the second to Botticelli. It seems that the person to ask Sandro was a member of the Vespucci family, who was patron of the church and whose house stood nearby; Botticelli, too, lived very close. It is probable that the paintings were executed at the same time, or at least, in the same year, as we know that between 1481 and 1482 Sandro, called to Rome to work on the decoration of the Sistine chapel, "lends" the same approach to the portrait of pope Sixtus II as he does for the Florentine fresco.
In 1564, according to the decree of the Council of Trent, the roodscreen was knocked down. The two frescos would have been destroyed with all the rest, if it hadn't been for Cosimo I who proved faithful to the memories of his family, deciding to save the works of artists who had been protected by his ancestors. He had the frescos detached and moved to the wall of the nave, where they still face one another today between the third and the fourth altar. The flood of 1966 only damaged them slightly, but inspired a complete and accurate restoration.
St. Augustine, wearing a bishop's robes but without the mitre – which is placed on a lower shelf – is depicted at his desk: according to the Renaissance custom, the books that stand on the two bookshelves at the back are placed face on; the open text on the top right can be identified as Euclid's *Elements*. In front of the book is a 24 hour clock; on the other side of the same plain, is an armillary sphere. Augustine's face is ecstatically pushed towards a source of light which comes from the left; his left hand holds the inkpot in which he has rested his pen; his right is spread over his heart, while his fingers are contracting due to his emotional state. A contemporary scholar, Roberts, has suggested the very credible theory that the portrait shows the culminating moment in the legend when, while the saint was writing to the dying Jerome, he saw the vision and heard the words.
This is one of the most virile and inspired works of Botticelli, which shows here, as Horne has also mentioned, that the artist studied the robust style of Andrea del Castagno in depth.

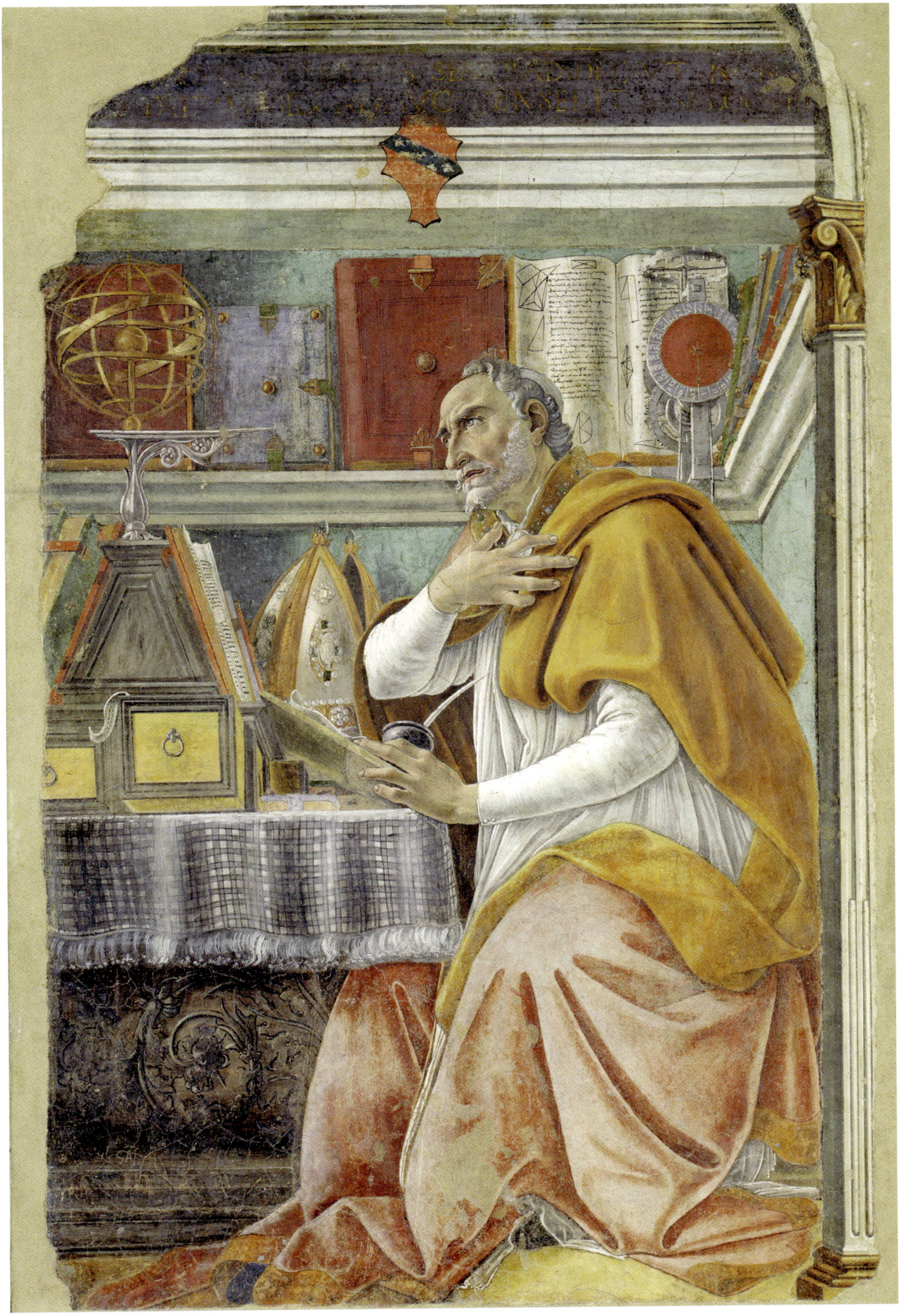

Vatican City

The frescos in the Sistine Chapel

The decoration of the Sistine Chapel took place against a backdrop of historical events which it is worth briefly recalling. Sixtus IV, who took the papal throne in 1471 (born Francesco della Rovere, 1414-1484) practiced a policy of open nepotism, to the particular benefit of Girolamo Riario, the son of his sister Bianca. In 1473, Girolamo was assigned the lordship of Imola, and four years later also the title of Forlì. This did not fail to worry the Florentines, who perceived a threat to their north-eastern borders. The situation worsened when Girolamo gave his support to the conspiracy that the Pazzi clan were organising against the Medici. On April 23, 1478, Lorenzo il Magnifico and his brother Giuliano were attacked in Santa Maria del Fiore; Giuliano was mortally wounded and Lorenzo only just survived. The Medici supporters then marched in arms on Palazzo Vecchio, where, according to a prearranged plan, other members of the group placed the *gonfaloniere* and his priors under arrest. The conspirators were seized, subjected to summary trials and executed. Among their leaders was Francesco Salviati, whom Pope Sixtus IV had appointed archbishop of Pisa four years before, with a specifically anti-Medici function. The execution of Salviati provoked the reaction of the pope, who excommunicated Florence and took up in arms with an ally, Ferdinand of Aragon, the King of Naples. Here Lorenzo resorted to a bold counter-offensive: risking his life, he went in person to Naples, where he conferred with Ferdinand, managing to win his respect. Deprived of his main support, the pope was forced to withdraw the interdict and restore diplomatic relations with Florence.

The process of reconciliation, however temporary, led to two Florentines boasting a privileged relationship with Pope Sixtus IV. One was Giovanni Tornabuoni, the all-powerful pope's treasurer; the other, the architect Giovannino de 'Dolci, was the commissioner of the apostolic Factories. Between 1477 and 1480, the Dolci clan had fully restored the Magna chapel (1277), which stood near the Vatican palaces, creating the current Sistine Chapel. As the pope wanted to commission an artistic decoration of great value, the city of Florence made its most eminent artists of the time available to the pontiff. This "embassy of the paintbrush" consisted of Cosimo Rosselli, Sandro Botticelli, Domenico Ghirlandaio, Piero di Cosimo and Pietro Perugino, accompanied by his student Pinturicchio. Later, Luca Signorelli also joined; Piermatteo Amelia was entrusted with the decoration of the vault (later painted by Michelangelo), depicting a starry sky.

Like almost all his other artistic companions, Sandro had to stay in Rome less than a year. In July 1481 Dolci asked each artist to produce a test fresco, which was to be examined and ultimately approved by the January of the following year. But the initial frescoes were so well received that as early as 27 October, contracts were signed stipulating that the painters and their assistants should complete all work by 15 March 1482. It appears that this deadline slipped by no more than two months, utterly negligible compared to the scale of the final masterpiece.

As has been noted, the chapel's decoration is structured in three sections. The first, corresponding to the bottom of the long walls of the chapel, consists of a succession of false curtains. The second is the main fresco cycle depicting the *Life of Moses* and the *Life of Christ*. Originally, this occupied all four walls: on the same wall as the altar a *Crucifixion* by Perugino was visible, removed fifty years later to make room for the *Universal Judgment*; on the entrance wall were a *Resurrection of Christ* by Ghirlandaio and the *Dispute over the body of Moses* by Signorelli, works which were both heavily repainted in the late sixteenth century. The third section depicts twenty-eight *Portraits of martyred popes*, where the full-figure pontiffs appear in pairs in the arches between the twelve windows that light the chapel. Other portraits from the same series, which continued in the upper part of the *Judgement* wall, have been lost.

Stories in the Old and New Testaments are seen in terms of perfect continuity, with Moses appearing as the foreshadowing of Christ. This reading was also meant to legitimise papal authority by affirming the direct line that, starting with Moses and Christ, passes through Peter and continues in the procession of pontiffs. Significant allusions to the temporal power of the Church are also present: in the background of the two main scenes of the *Lives* (*Christ giving the Keys to St. Peter* by Perugino and Botticelli's *Punishment*

of the Rebels) we can see the arch of Constantine, the emperor whose legendary "donation of Sutri" had made the papal throne the rightful heir of the Roman state.
Both the *Stories* and the papal portraits were executed as frescoes, but - to eliminate the differences in colour that emerged between one "day" and another and also to correct the wall's defects - the artists often resorted, as Michelangelo would later do, to applying layers of dry tempera. The work of assistants is conspicuous, particularly in the portraits, even if Botticelli made much less use of them than the others.

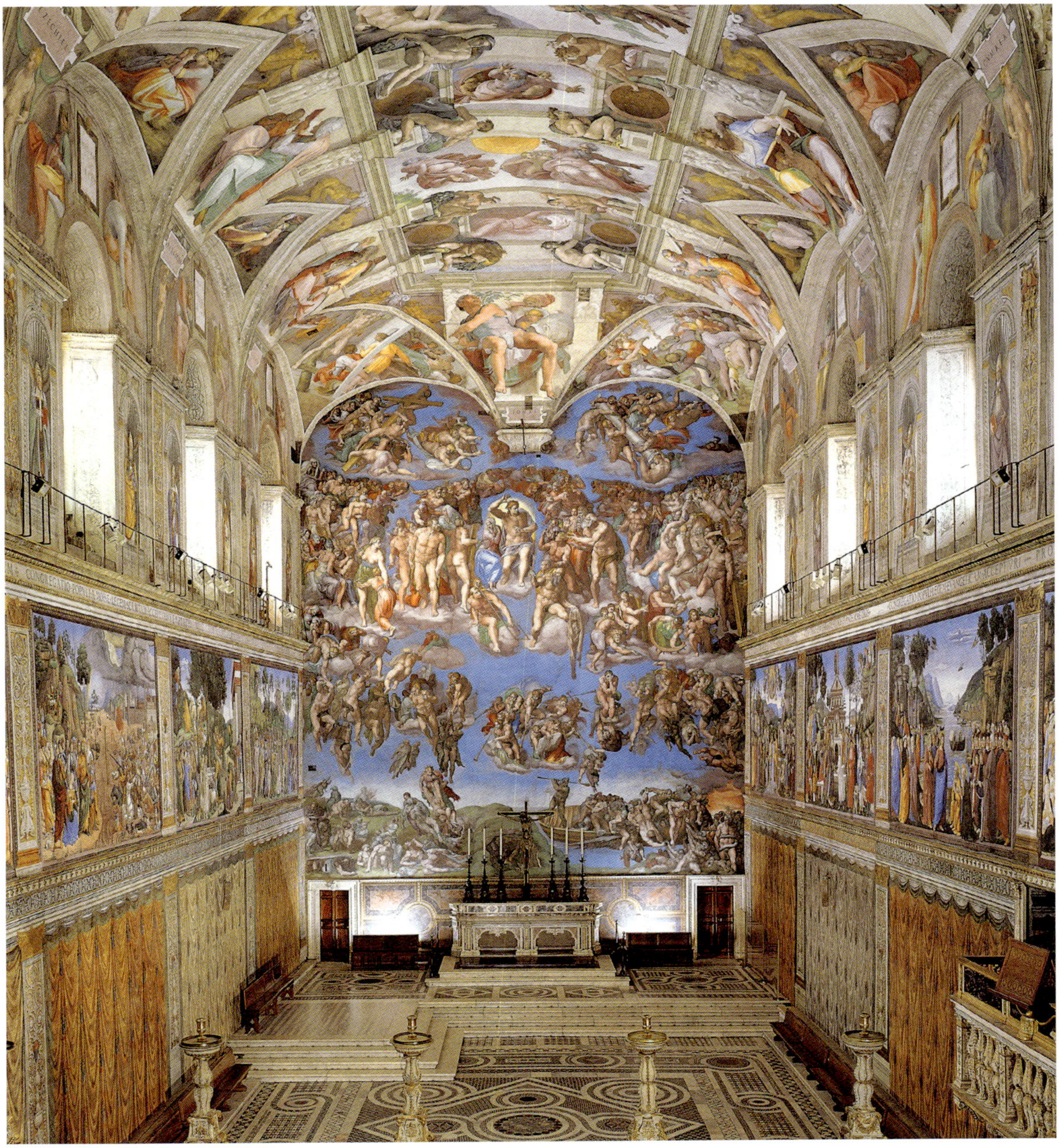

TRIALS OF MOSES
1481-82, fresco, 348.5 x 558 cm

These *Trials of Moses* are the counterpart to the *Trials of Christ* also painted by Sandro. They appear in one big fresco, presenting with great compositional skill seven episodes from the life of young Moses taken from the book of *Exodus*. In the foreground, on the right, Moses kills an Egyptian who is beating a Jew; knowing he has been discovered, he flees to the country of Madian, and while resting on the edge of a well, he sees the daughters of the priest Jethro that come to draw water to give to their flock. A group of pastors that want to stop them arrive, but Moses drives them away (back, centre) and helps the girls to draw water (centre). After having joined Jethro's family, through marriage to his daughter Zipporah, they graze their flocks and lead them beyond the desert, beneath Mount Horeb. Here he sees the burning bush, and takes off his shoes to enter; God speaks to him (left, top) ordering him to return to Egypt with his family to free the Jews from slavery. Moses obeys and, at the head of his family, starts out on the journey (foreground, left). According to some – although a less likely interpretation – this last scene instead shows the exodus of the Israelites from Egypt.

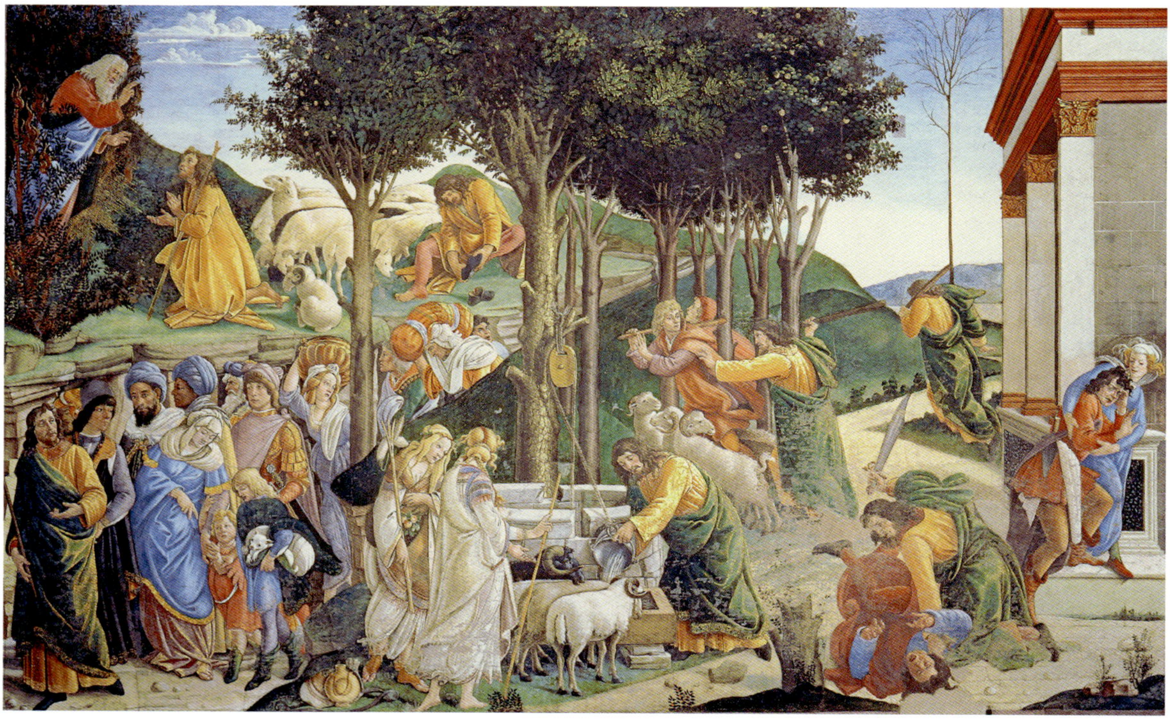

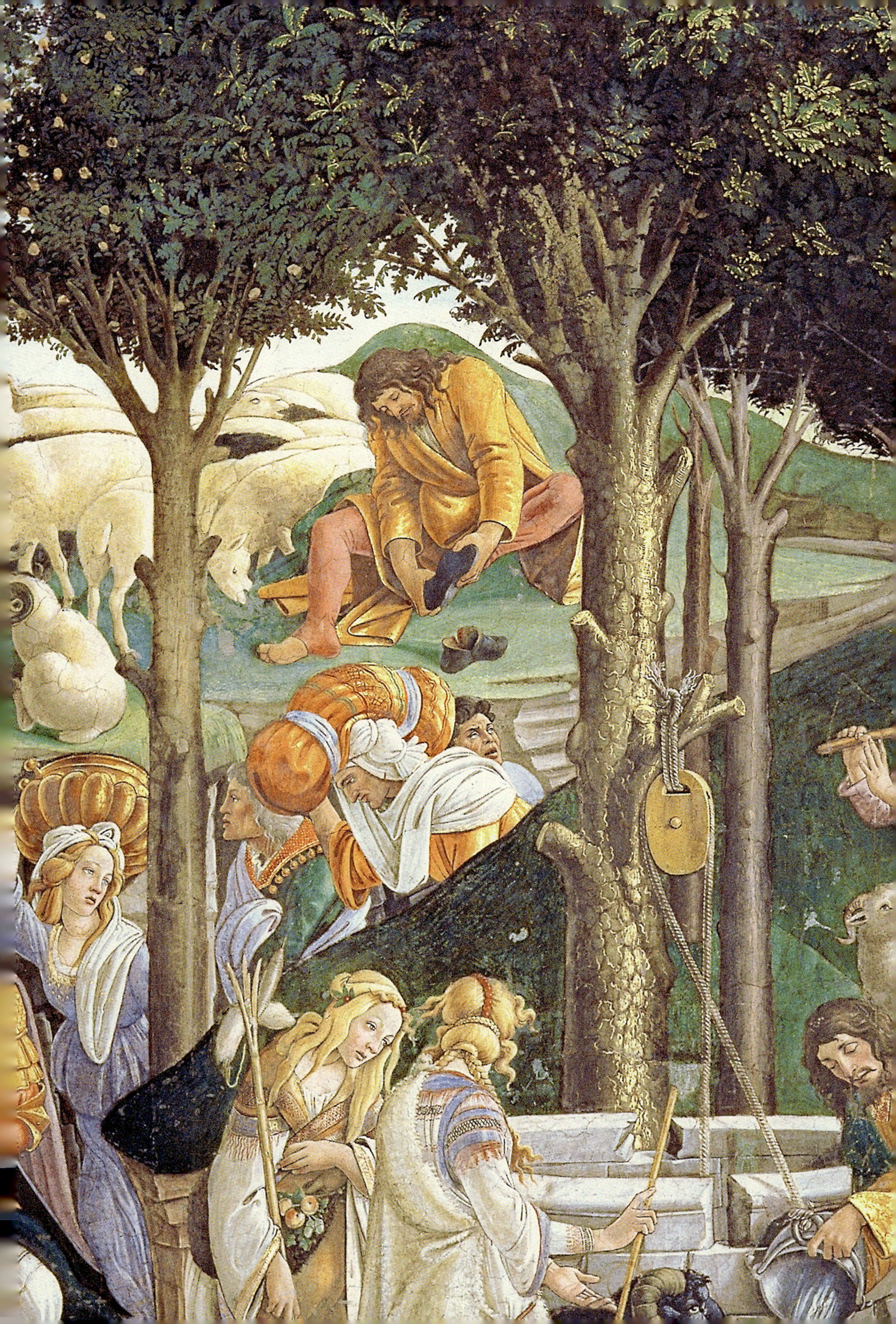

TRIALS OF CHRIST
1481-82, fresco, 345.5 x 555 cm

Undertaken by Botticelli in July 1481, this fresco (also known by the name of its central episode, *Purification of the lepers*) is the third in the cycle of *Stories from the New Testament*.
Satan's endeavours to tempt Christ three times (*Mt.*, 4) are depicted in the background, where the demon curiously appears in Franciscan robes. It has been suggested that this inappropriate garb represents a satirical dig by Sandro towards Sixtus IV, who before rising to the papal throne had been the general of the Franciscans. Rather than improbable, the theory is quite absurd: simply, the artist is underlining the paradoxical shape-shifting power of the devil, indirectly celebrating the Order founded by the friar of Assisi. Satan challenges Jesus, who is fasting in the desert, to turn stones into bread to ease his hunger; at the centre, we see the two figures on the top of the Temple of Jerusalem, from which the devil tries to tempt the Saviour to throw himself; then he shows the Son of God the magnificence of worldly wealth and offers them to him (*top, right*), but Jesus refuses and throws him down from the mountain, forcing him to show his real aspect, while three angels prepare the table, foreshadowing the Eucharistic sacrifice. Having beaten the temptations of Satan, Jesus (*above, left*) sees the leper healed, and sends him to the priest (*Mt.*, 8,1-4). The presence of three angels, to whom he seems to explain what is happening centre stage, places the laid table in parallel with the purification ceremony, which was also carried out with the blood of a sacrificial lamb. (*Lev.*, 14,14). The high priest receives the offer (the basin full of blood) from the hand of the healed leper, while the faithful make votive gifts of animals and bundles of firewood. It is a clear reference to the crucifixion of Jesus, who by his death, offers his own flesh and blood for the redemption of mankind. At the front are a wide range of characters, whose faces are so clearly drawn that it becomes evident that they are kinds of portraits. In particular, we can apparently identify Girolamo Riario, Giuliano della Rovere (the future Pope Julius II), the King of Naples Ferdinand of Aragon, Botticelli himself (far left) and Filippino Lippi (next to him). The fresco also contains two celebrative allusions: the Roman Temple is modelled on the hospital of Santo Spirito, which was built at the same time as the painting was completed, while the two large oak trees are a clear reference to the arms of the delle Rovere family.

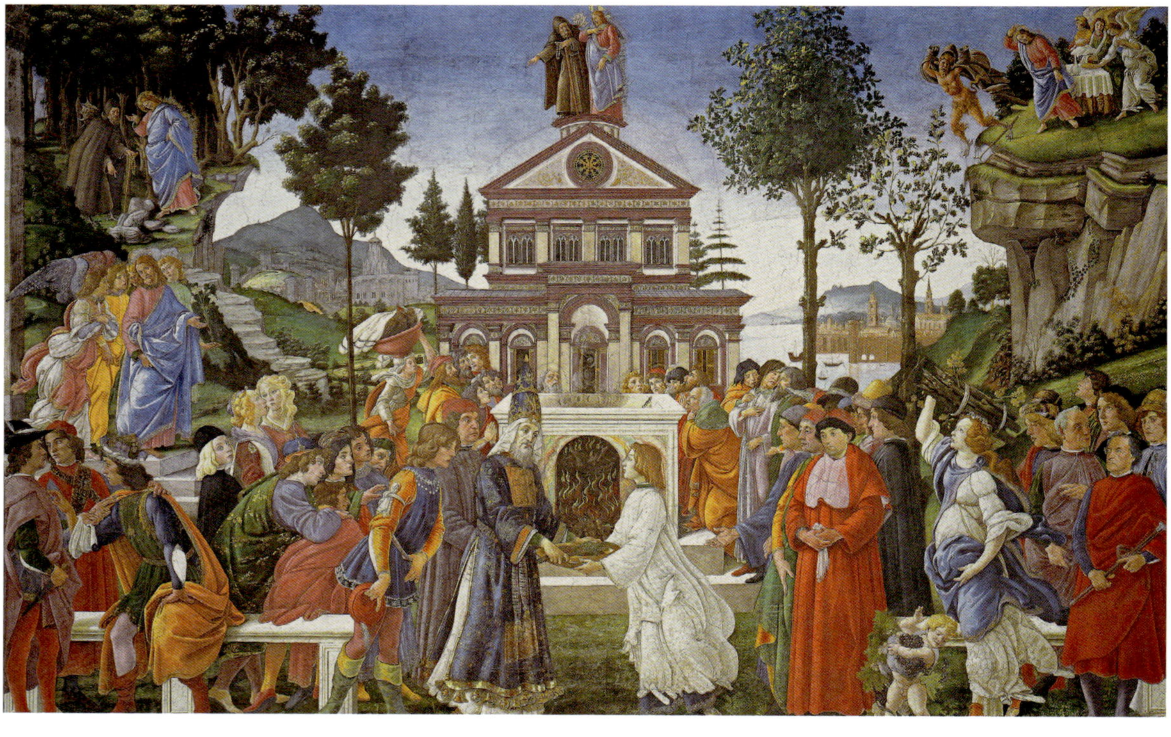

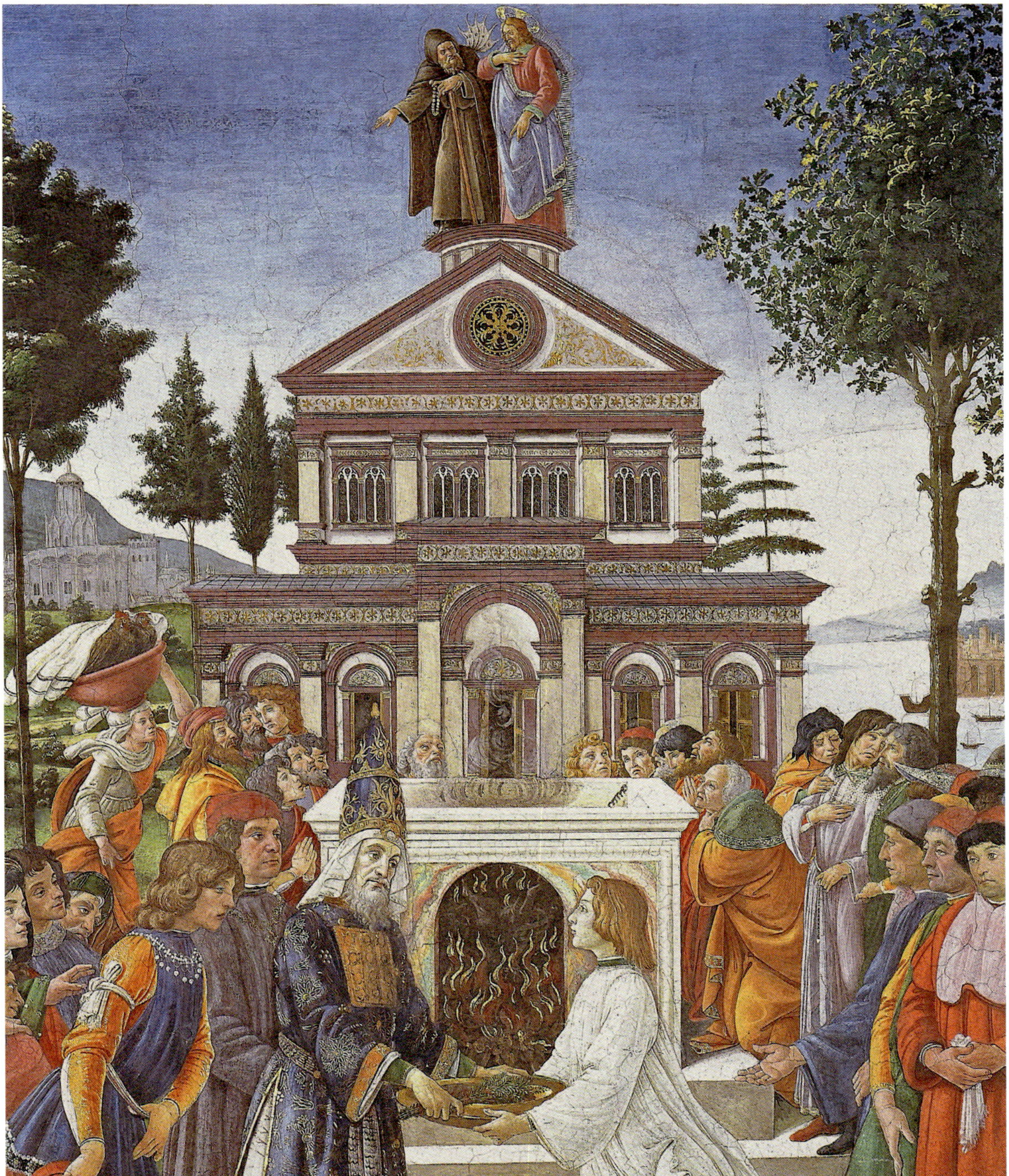

Punishment of the Rebels
1481-82, fresco, 348.5 x 570 cm

This work – which reveals the intervention of Sandro's assistants particularly in the architecture and the urban landscape to the right – is the counterpart to Perugino's *Delivery of the keys*. According to the bible story *(Nm, 16, 1-35)*, Korah, Dathan and Abiram tried to rally the people against the priest, Aaron. After praying, Moses sets a test: the rebels and Aaron have their censers placed on the altar of God, which cannot fail to indicate a preference over one or the other. The test reveals God's favour lies with Aaron, and Moses punishes the rebels. On the right, Achariot restrains the angry crowd, who are clutching rocks for the stoning, while Moses addresses them. In the centre, the priests carry out the test on Moses' invitation: the smoke from Aaron and Eleazar's censers rises to heaven, while those of Korah, Dathan and Abiram shoot out tongues of flame towards them, and they fall; on the left, Moses sends them alive into *sheol*, i.e. hell, while Eldad and Medad, the sons of Aaron, miraculously levitate.
The centre of the composition is dominated by the arch of Constantine in Rome, which bears on its central stone the following inscription: NEMO SIBI ASSVMM/AT HONOREM NISI / VOCATVS A DEO / TANQVAM ARON, meaning "Let no man take the honour unto himself except he that is called by God, as Aaron was." The ruins of classical construction on the right are identified as the so-called Septizonium (the palace on the Palatine Hill built in 203 AD by the emperor Septimius Severus and demolished by Pope Sixtus V in 1588).
The content of the epigraph and the tiara on the head of Aaron also allude to an incident contemporary to the drawing of the fresco. A few months before, Andreas Zamometic, the archbishop of Kranj in Slovenia, had harshly criticised the work of Sixtus IV (whom he defined as *filius Diaboli*, "son of the devil") and the customs of the Roman curia. Arrested in June 1481, Zamometic was deposed from his position as imperial legate; on his release two months later, he continued his work as an anti-Roman propagandist in Germany, where he was able to benefit from the implicit support of Emperor Frederick III of Habsburg.
This picture also features realistic portraits, even if we cannot be totally clear about their identification. On the far right, the first figure above Moses could be Alessandro Farnese (later Pope Paul III), the second carries the likeness of the artist and the third appears to be the humanist Pomponio Leto.

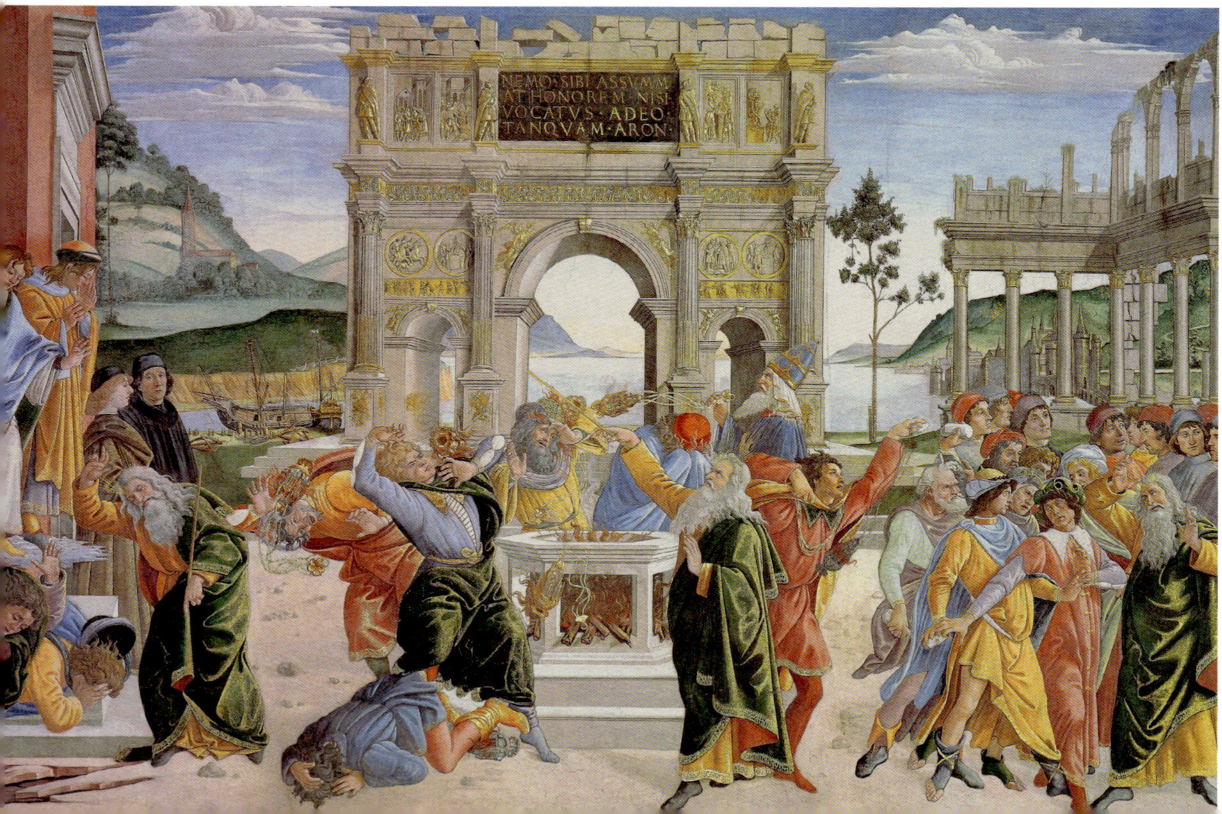

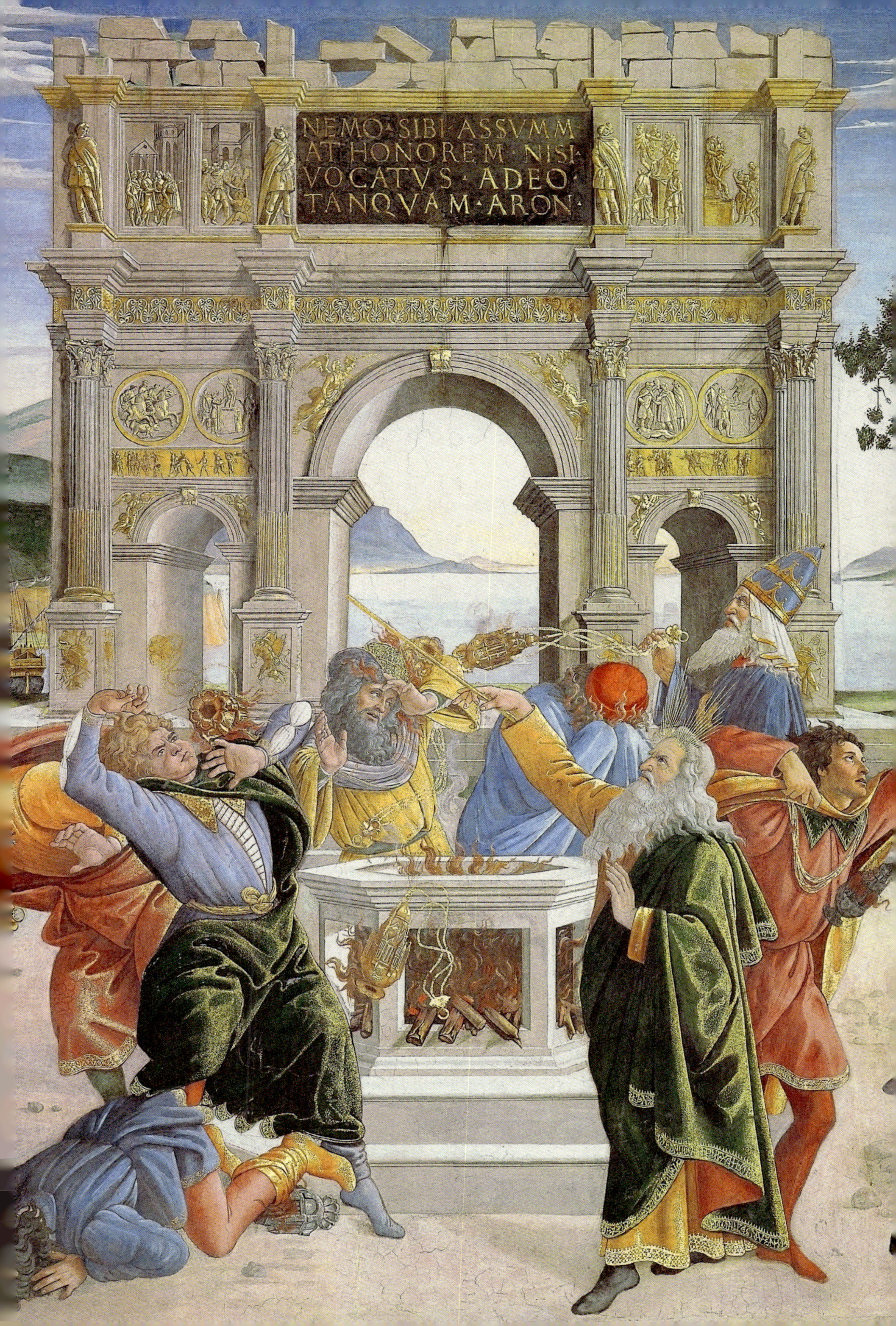
NEMO·SIBI·ASSVMM
AT HONOREM·NISI·
VOCATVS·ADEO
TANQVAM·ARON·

Milan

Museo Poldi Pezzoli

Pietà (Deposition in the tomb)
late fifteenth century, tempera on panel, 107 x 71 cm

This work is almost certainly the *Pietà* that Vasari defines as "very beautiful", which was originally found in the Florentine church of Santa Maria Maggiore, next to the Panciatichi chapel.
Its dimensions are explained by the fact that the work, just like the *St. Sebastian* (see p. 68) which was kept for a time in the same church, was fixed to a pillar of the pulpit, above the altar of the chapel of the Pietà. Towards the end of the fifteenth century the patronage of the chapel belonged to the illuminator Donato Antonio 0Cioni, whose family, it is documented, included followers of Savonarola. In 1629 the new patron, Jacopo Viviani, demolished the altar and the painting was moved to the sacristy, where its presence is documented again in 1755. The Milanese collector Poldi Pezzoli bought it in 1855.
Starting with Horne, the author of the first major biography of Botticelli (1908), scholars have long believed that this was an old copy; but the careful restoration done in 1951 revealed elements which confirmed the work's origins in Sandro's mature phase.The scene takes place before the door of the tomb, and has seven figures forming a kind of pyramid, whose apex is Nicodemus (Jn. 19:39). He looks to the sky with both hands raised to show off the symbols of the Passion: in his right he holds a crown made of thorns, with the nails of the cross in his left; in a sign of respect, direct contact with the relics is prevented by two translucent veils. Beneath him is St. John, with his chin resting on the temple of the Virgin Mary, who holds the body of Jesus on her lap, almost in a crouching position; of the two women flanking the Madonna (Mary Magdalene, and Mary of Cleophas, *Mk.* 14:40), the one on the right lovingly holds the head of the Saviour; lower left, a third woman, the prone Mary Magdalene, embraces the feet of Christ and rests her head on them with a loving gesture. The extremely skilled composition exploits the equilibrium between its two vertical lines and its central circle. The first vertical line starts from Nicodemus' right arm, and continues in the arm of St. John and that of the Madonna; the second procedes from the left arm of Nicodemus, continuing through the head of the feminine figure and the head of Jesus. The circle, meanwhile, starts from the head of St. John, continuing through the three female heads and closes with the curved line of the body of Christ.
It has been argued that the exaggerated elongation of the Virgin's lap and the strange posture of the Saviour (who couldn't physically be carried on his mother's knee) as well as the "impossible" curve of Mary Magdalene's neck were proof that this was not Botticelli's work. But in his latter phase, Sandro put aside pure naturalism in favour of narrative pathos; hence the labelling of the mature Botticelli as a "proto-mannerist".

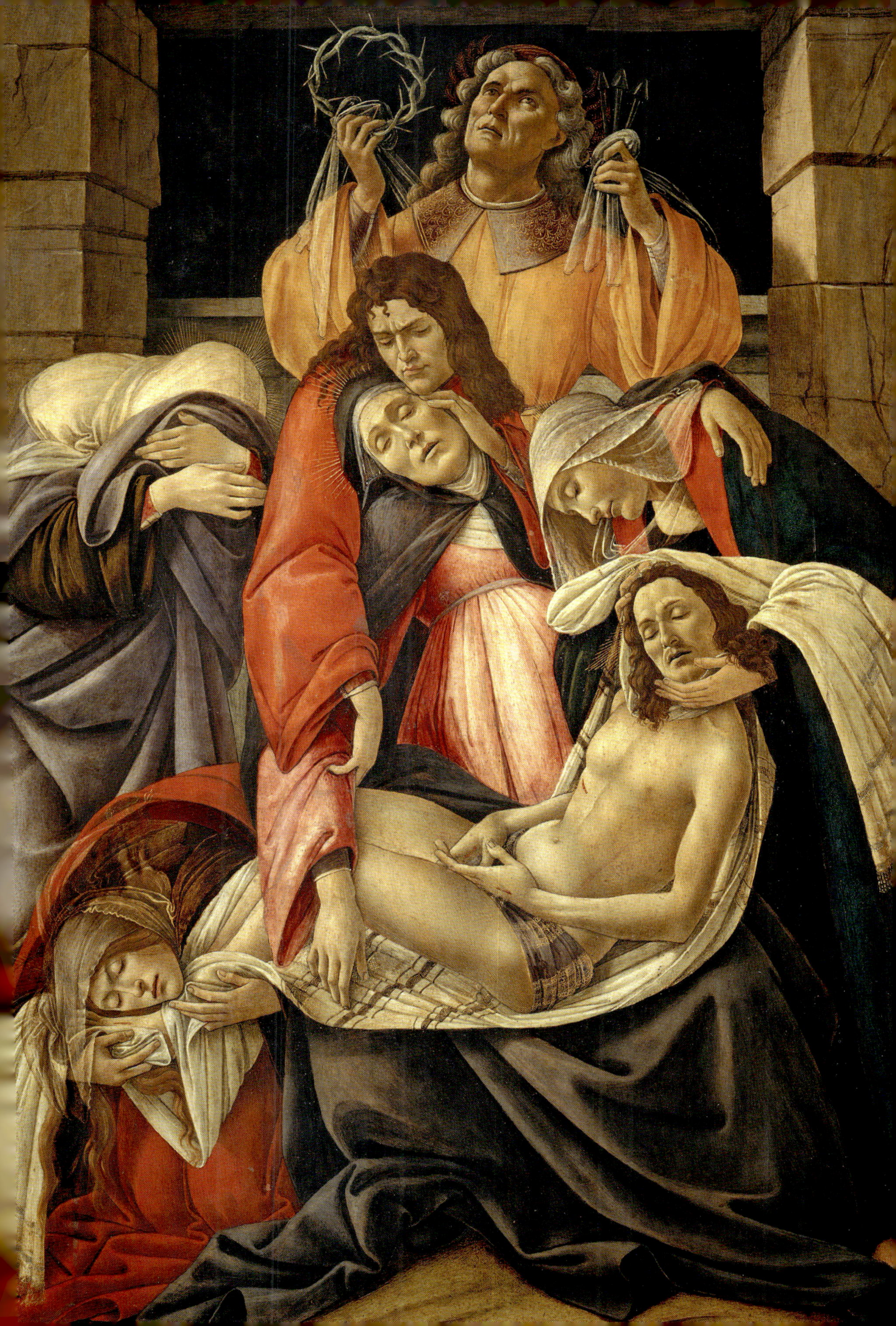

MADONNA OF THE BOOK

c. 1483, tempera on panel, 58 x 39.5 cm

In Poldi Pezzoli's collection, this painting was already officially catalogued as authored by Sandro in 1881; however, a series of retouches, changes and corrections added over the centuries made it difficult to fully appreciate the work, and brought some to the conclusion that it was a product of his workshop. An accurate restoration in 1951, however, removed most doubts about its provenance. Apart from a few rare exceptions, the scholars have also been in agreement about its date, placing it somewhere between 1481 and 1485.
As its modest size would suggest, this is a devotional work for private use, a fact also signalled by its rectangular shape - a form almost never used for Botticelli's Madonnas of the 1480s.
Mary, with the Child in her arms, sits in a corner of the room, facing a window that frames a serene sky; the only landscape detail is a clump of low trees on the far right.
The Child, with his eyes raised towards his mother, carries a crown of thorns on his left arm, and holds three small nails in his hand, foreshadowing the Passion. The Virgin's right hand reaches out towards a book whose few words have allowed us to identify it as a Book of Hours.
There are some particularly splendid details, such as the real and proper still life of fruit, with its almost Flemish execution, and the casket on which it rests. The process of restoration has brought to light the precious gold filigree which decorates garments and objects in the painting, helping to give the work a genuine luminosity.

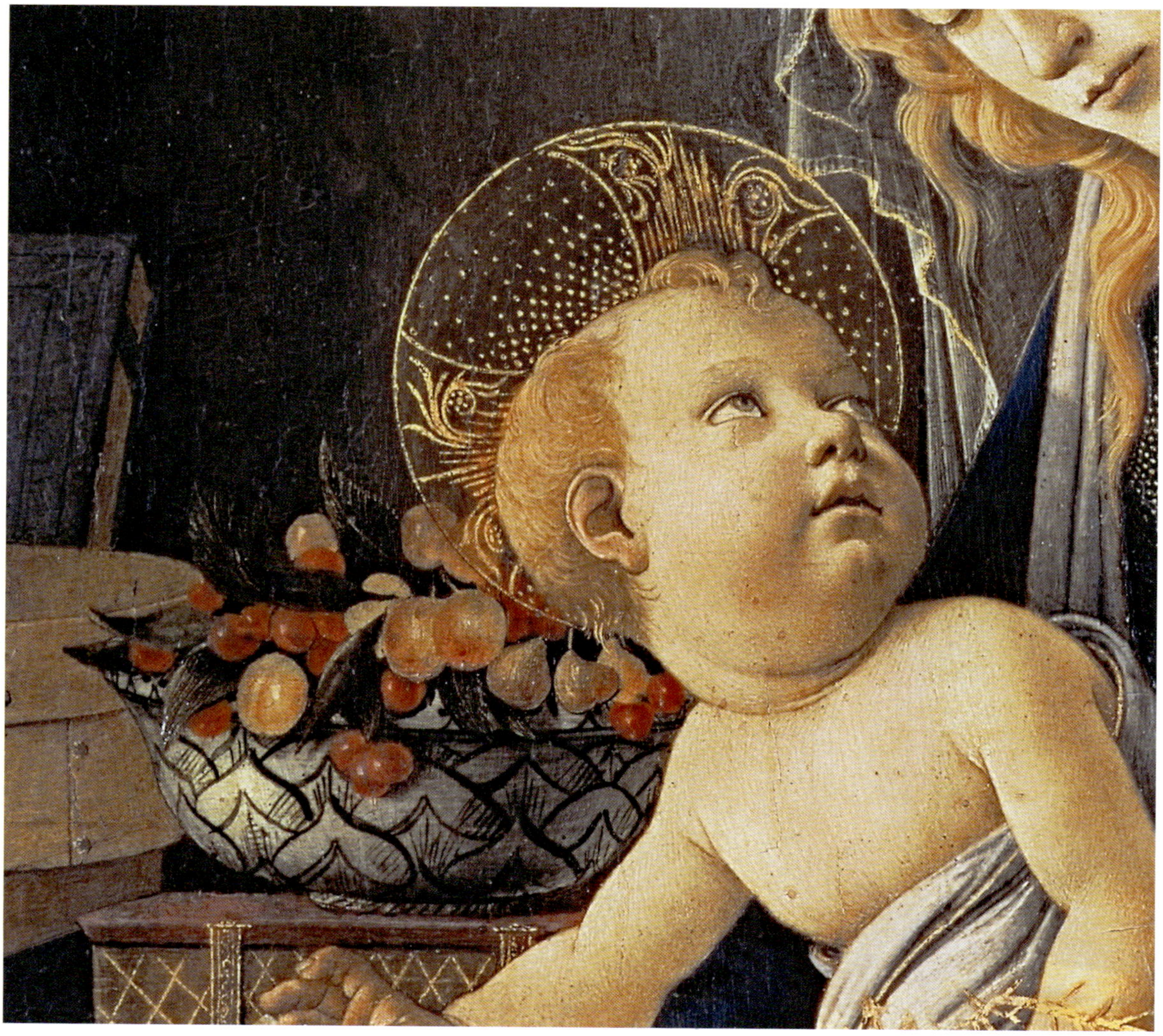

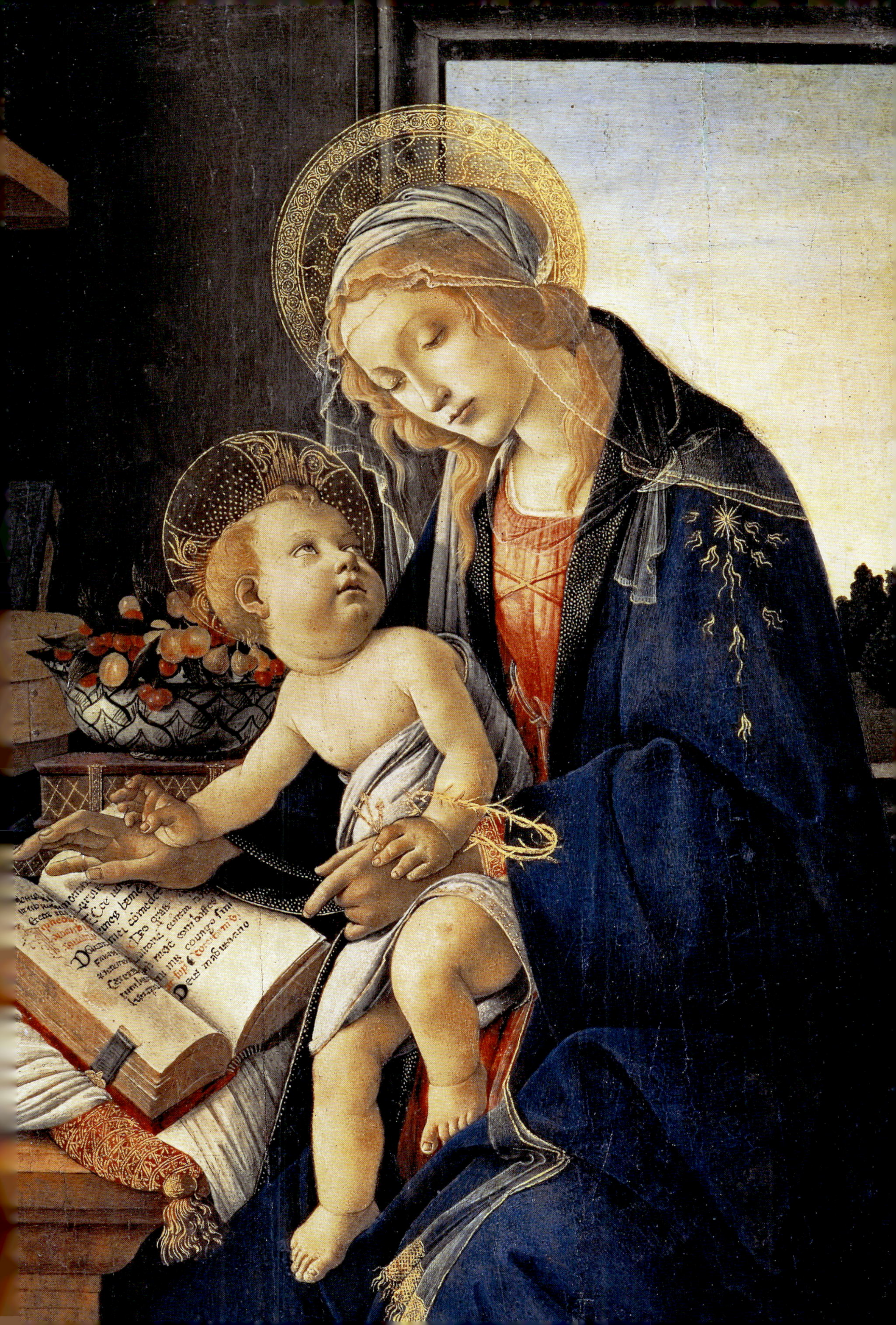

London

The National Gallery

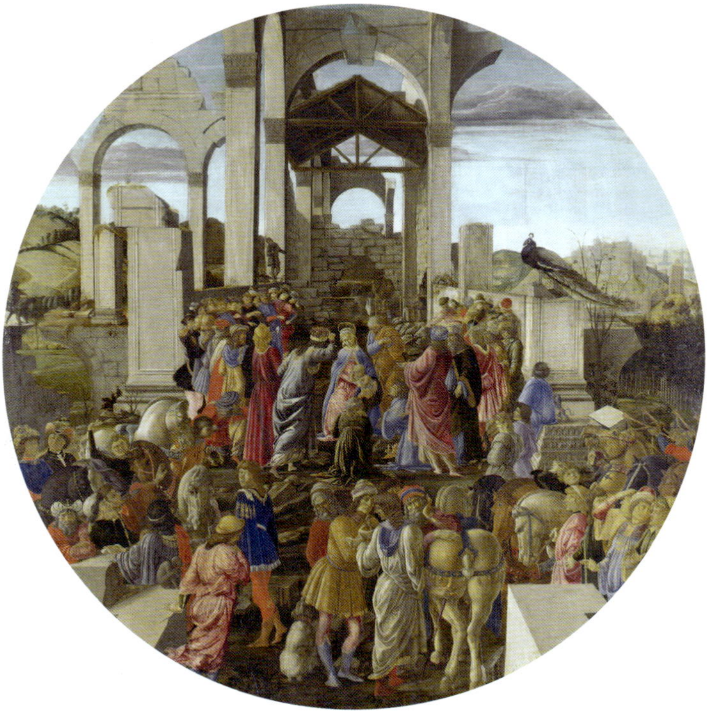

Adoration of the Magi
1473, tempera on panel, ∅ cm 131,5

In the second edition of the *Lives* (1568), Vasari states he has seen this *tondo* at the house of the Pucci clan. Indeed, it is still mentioned in a family inventory of 1698, but by 1720, has passed into the ownership of the Guicciardini family, along with the rest of the goods of Luisa Ninfa de' Pucci. In the eighteenth century, it is sold to an English collector; in England it would be the subject of various transactions, before reaching its present home. Noting the pseudo-classical ruins in the background which are out of proportion with respect to the rest of the work, the theory goes that this was a birthing tray or "desco da parto", a large wooden plate, round or many sided, which was used for collecting small gifts destined for a woman who was about to give birth. Indeed, looking at it laid flat, almost "skimming with the eyes" (Mandel), the painting's proportions make more sense; only that its dimensions seem rather exaggerated for an object of that nature, of which many examples have survived but which rarely exceed 60cm in diameter; it also appears to be missing on its base the heraldic marks which were almost always included. Perhaps the circular work was made to be looked at from the bottom upwards, even inserted in an architectural frame: this would have a flattening effect, which is almost better. One way or the other, we seem to be looking at the first example of anamorphosis in the West, even pre-dating Leonardo's experiments. For the first time, Sandro creates an *Adoration* in which the figures are depicted centrally and not to one side. In the richness of their costumes, in the variety of the faces and their attitudes we can already see the signs of great mastery, even if the scene tends to fragment into many smaller episodes that reduce the dramatic impact of the whole work.The young man in the foreground next to the horse, with his face turned towards the viewer, is perhaps a self-portrait. As far as the symbolic aspects of the painting go, the "classical" temple in ruins is an allegory for the pagan world which has been destroyed by the coming of Christ: according to a medieval legend, at the birth of Jesus, the ancient temple of Peace in Rome suddenly collapsed.

The enormous peacock perched on the wall on the right, meanwhile, is a symbol of resurrection, as it was thought that the bird's flesh was incorruptible.

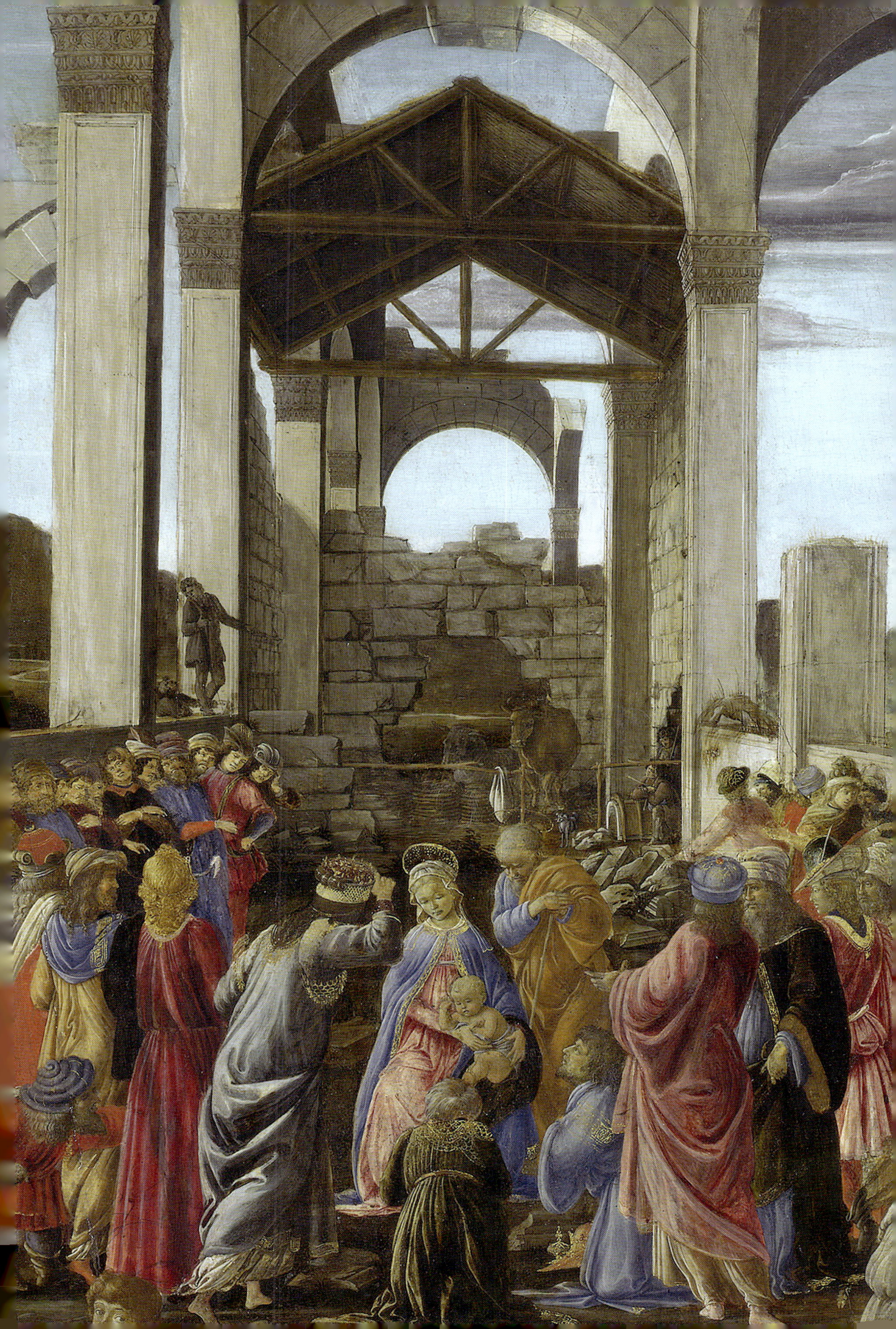

Venus and Mars

1483, tempera on panel, 69 x 173.5 cm

Bought in Florence by Sir Alexander Barker around 1865, this work passed into the hands of the National Gallery in 1874. An accurate restoration in 1943 liberated it of the countless retouches which had obscured many of its details. The dimensions of the panel lend support to the hypothesis that this may have been a *spalliera* or backboard (see p. 72), and that the subject portrayed may have been of an auspicious nature on the occasion of a marriage. It was Gombrich, commenting on the detail of the wasps which swarm out of a tree stump in the top right-hand corner, who first suggested the theory that the sponsor could have come from the Vespucci family, which had the coat of arms of "a red field crossed with a blue band and a procession of golden wasps". The scene takes place within a wood, where we can see laurel and myrtle trees. On the left, Venus – who wears a light, white dress bordered with gold and has her hair bound in long plaits which meet at her breast, just as we have already seen in the *Primavera* – lies semi-reclined, with her right arm resting on a cushion. Her face, in which we can read an almost imperceptible note of irony, is turned towards the face of Mars, who is also half-lying down and in an almost symmetrical position with respect to Venus. The young god, portrayed as nude with a white cloth around his waist, has his head thrown back as he enjoys a deep sleep, heavy lidded and with mouth half-open.

His war-like attributes, which are depicted (the tournament lance, helmet with visor, the sword with the crossed hilt, the armour), are in the hands of a group of chubby and playful satyrs in the background: one

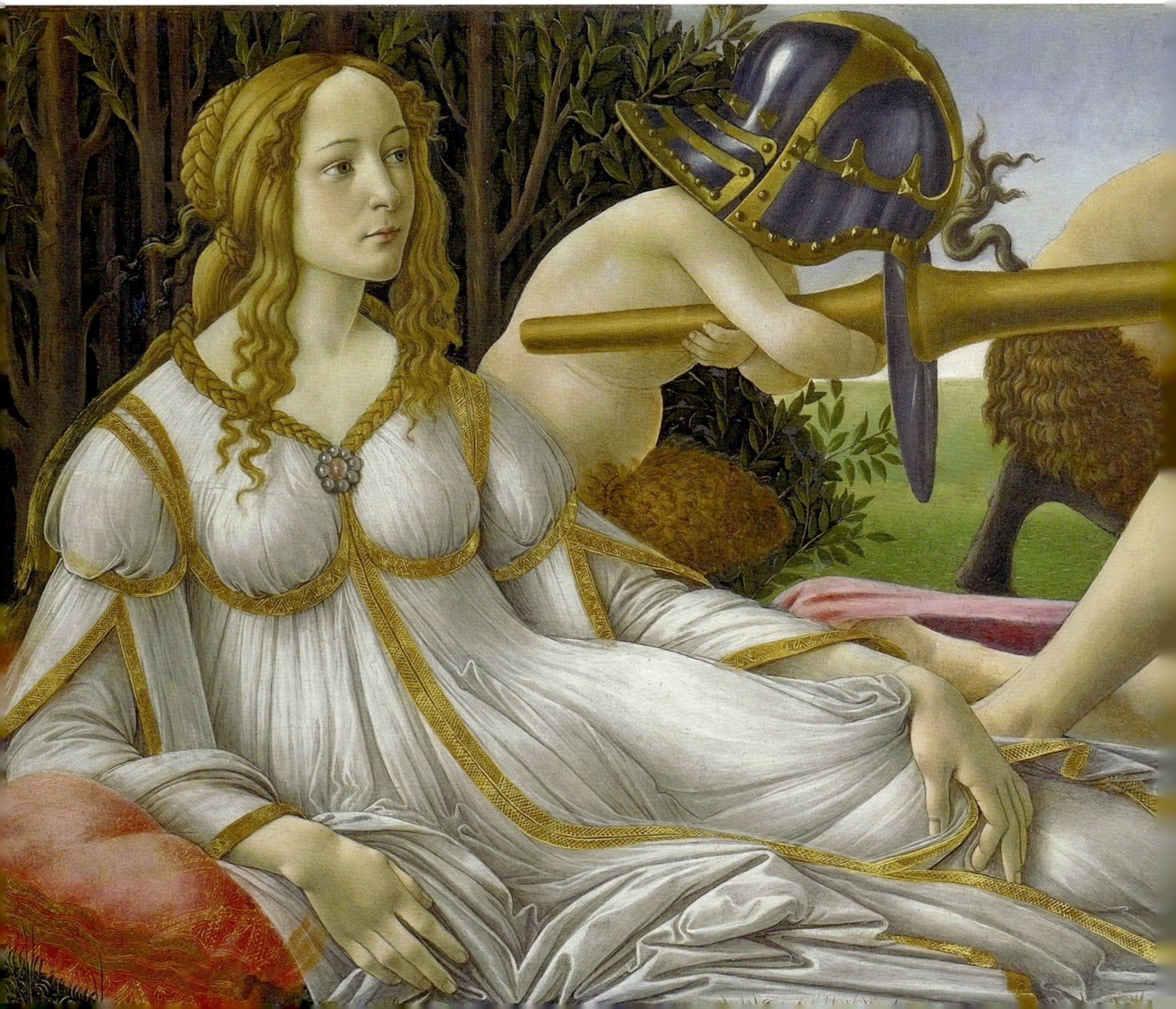

has perched the helmet on his head and grips the lance, supported by another; a third is huffing and puffing right in the ear of the sleeping figure; a fourth has managed to crawl into the armour, and sliding behind Mar's back, tries to get the sword which has been abandoned in the grass.

The work can also be appreciated in its captivating light-heartedness without reference to the symbols of Neo-Platonism. However, there is also a hint of the *Symposium* of Marsilio Ficino, in which Venus' superiority, as the symbol of love and concord is upheld over that of Mars, the symbol of hate and discord. We are back again at the Venus-*Humanitas* of *Primavera* and the *Birth of Venus*; the god of war has been overcome by virtue of the *Discordia concors* which, causing the attraction of opposites, finishes with the triumph of goodness. The literary fonts for the scene include the major and minor classics, such as Lucretius and Reposianus (*De concubitu Martis et Veneris*, III century A.D.) and authors contemporary to Botticelli, such as Poliziano (*Stanze per la giostra*) and Lorenzo il Magnifico (*Hymn to Mars and Venus*). Some scholars have also psychoanalysed the work, starting from the same sources and particularly with reference to Lucretius (*De Rerum Natura*, I, vv. 36-41), seeing Mar's slumber as a post-coital nap, and the lance and sword as phallic symbols. Symbols which "have both fallen down, and the cupids play with them. The lance, symbol of virility, has been taken from Mars, and in fact is now directed from her towards him" (Cano Alonso and Martínez Gázquez, 2001).

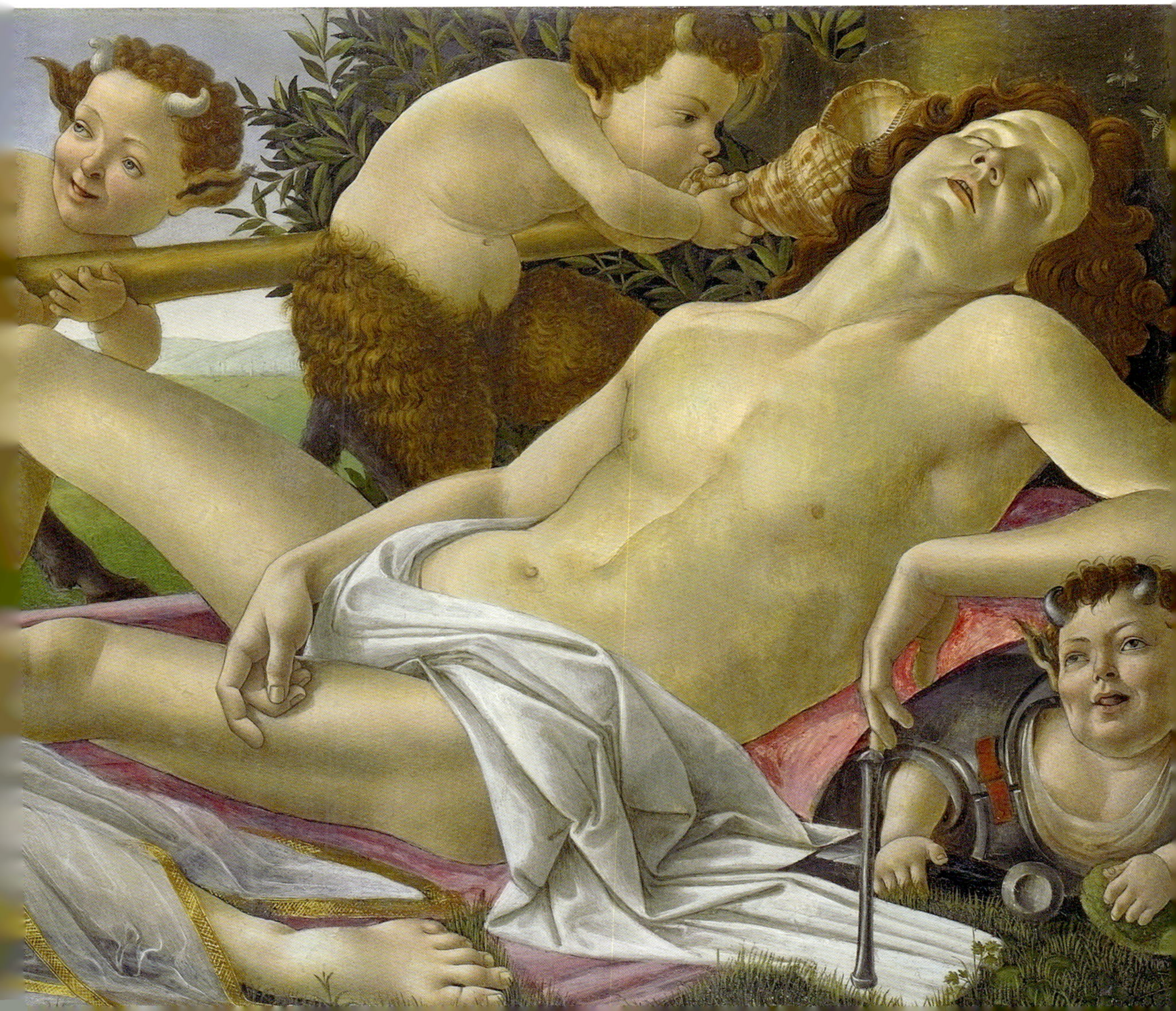

MYSTIC NATIVITY

1501, tempera on canvas, 108.5 x 75 cm

This work, which belonged to the Aldobrandini family, was moved to Rome when a branch of that clan set up home there. Around 1800, the furnishings of Villa Aldobrandini were dispersed, and the painting was bought by the English collector W.Y. Ottley, who took it home. After various sales it was eventually acquired by the National Gallery in 1878. The centre of the composition is filled with a canopy which leads into a rocky cavern. On each side are angels who present the humbly dressed Magi (on the left) and the shepherds (on the right). At the bottom, in the foreground, three angels dressed in green, white and red embrace three men; seven little devils poke out from the cracks in the rock behind them. On the roof, three winged creatures kneel, in clothes that echo the colours worn by the angels at the front; the central figure, in red, holds a book, supported by the other two. At the top, against the sky, a theatrical carousel recalls the sacred symbols: it is a ring of 12 angels that carry streamers, crowns and olive branches, whose garments echo the white, red and the green. The olive is another constant in the work: the Magi are crowned with it, as are the shepherds and the men in the foreground, just as all the creatures in the sky clutch olive branches. At the top of the painting, on three lines, is a Greek epigram: "I, Alessandro, painted this picture towards the end of the year 1500, during the disturbances in Italy, in the half time after the time, according to the XI [chapter] of St. John in the second war of the Apocalypse, during the three and a half year liberation of the Devil; it shall then be chained according to the XII [chapter] and we shall see him fall as in this painting".

The epigram helps us date and interpret the work. In Florence, as in other cities, the year started *ab incarnatione Domini* (i.e. from March 25th, the feast of the Annunciation) so the end of 1500 would have corresponded with the first few months of 1501. In that period, there were many "disturbances in Italy", starting with the death of il Magnifico (1492) and the fall of Charles VIII of France, with the subsequent expulsion of the Medicis from Florence (1494); and, even closer to the date of the painting, the trial and death of Savonarola (1498), the conquest of Lombardy by Louis XII (1499), the threats against Florence by Cesare Borgia, son of Pope Alessandro VI, who set him up as ruler of Romagna (in January 1501 he laid siege to Faenza, which fell in March)...

The two biblical references on the other hand allude to the occupation of the Holy City by the gentiles for 42 months (*Rev.* 11:2); to the triumph of Archangel Michael, who, with his celestial troops defeated and hurled to the earth "the dragon" Satan and his demons (*Rev.* 12:7-9).

The expression "in the half time after the time" echoes on the other hand a third passage by St. John (*Rev.*12,14), where 42 months, or three and a half years, are defined as "a time, two times and half a time". It therefore means "half way through the year after the first three and a half years", or "a year and a half after the start of the fatal time" (that which Sandro and / or his sponsors would see as "the liberation of the Devil".)

The event which would have signalled the start of the 42 bleak months is usually identified as the death of Savonarola, by whom Sandro had been deeply influenced for some time. In that case, seeing that the Dominican was executed on May 23rd 1498, the painting, completed around a year and a half later, would have meant some 13 or 14 months of work. The allusion to *Revelation* is telling: it is no coincidence that Savonarola dedicated around 42 sermons to the theme, today lost. Its also worth highlighting the use of Greek: the author or the translator of the epigram – almost certainly a surviving member of the circle of il Magnifico – sought, alongside Sandro, to stress the religious sense as much as possible of a work which celebrated the ideas of Savonarola, in particular the coming of the new Nazareth, in which the friar had sought to transform Florence. The three winged created on the roof of the shed are the theological virtues, Faith (white), Hope (green) and Charity (red); their representations at the bottom allude, in the embrace with the three male figures, to their triumph in the world of men and the defeat of sin (the devils which hide in the ground symbolise the seven capital sins).

In the context of Botticelli's work, this painting marks his abandonment of the use of rational perspective: the figures, shown in rigid, "iconic" poses, are actually created in inverse proportions of size (if we compare the image of the Virgin to those of the characters in the foreground, and even more the forms above of the oversized angels).

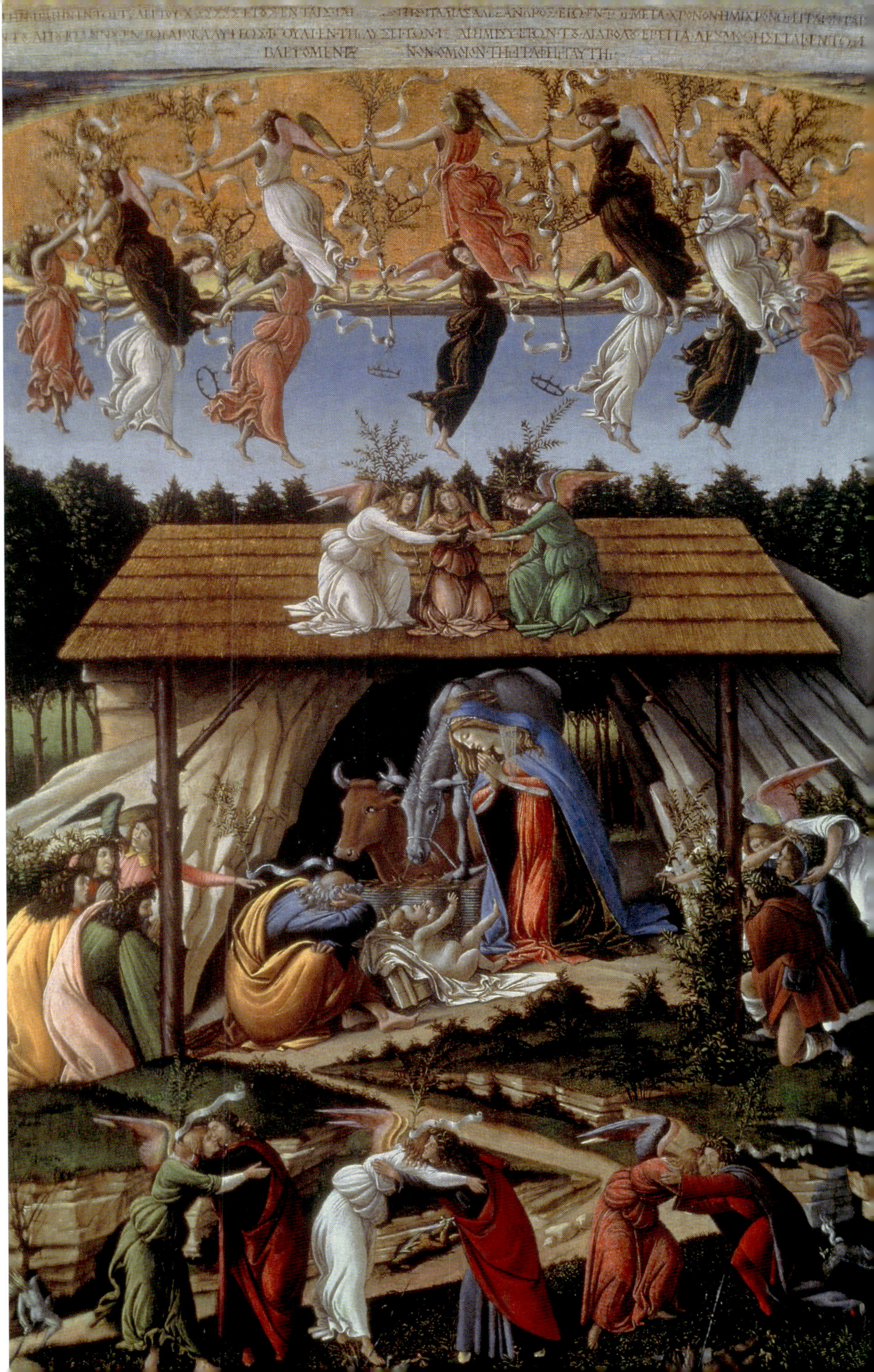

Berlin

Staatliche Museen Preussischer Kulturbesitz, Gemäldegalerie

Saint Sebastian

1473, tempera on shaped panel, 195 x 75 cm

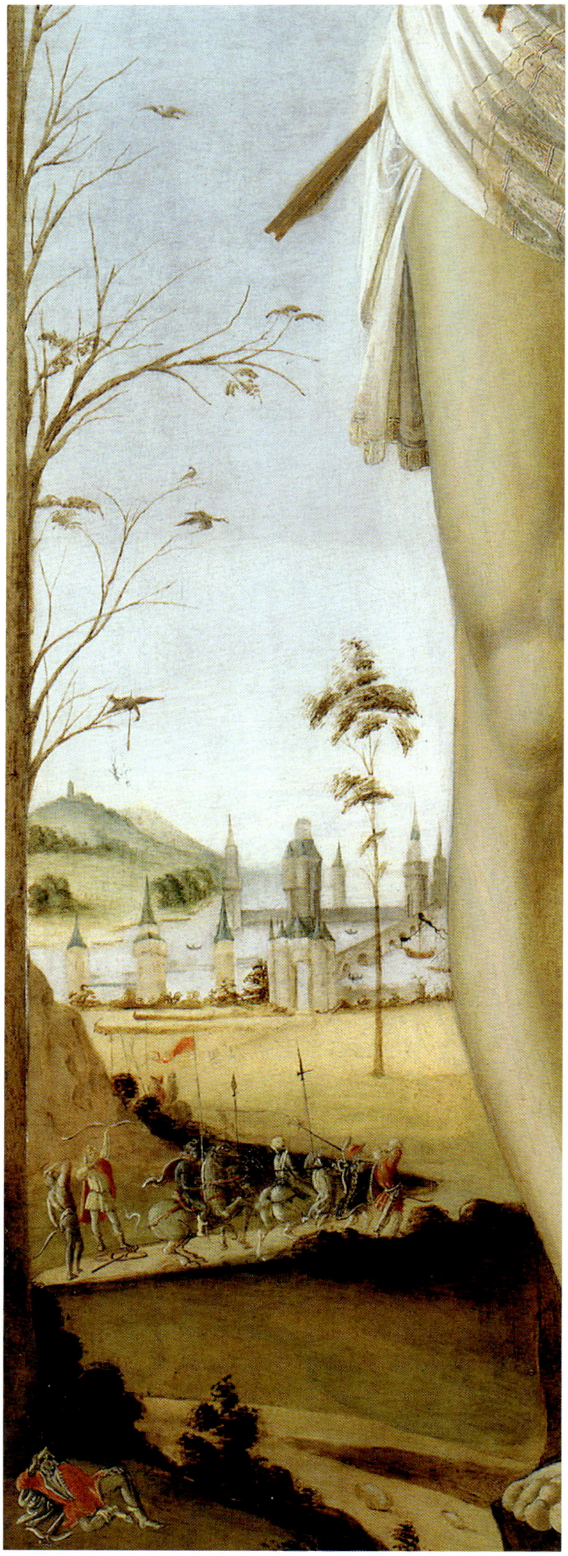

When this work reached Berlin in 1821, along with other works from the Solly collection, it was attributed to Piero del Pollaiolo; but in 1864, Cavalcaselle credited it to Botticelli, not only from a close stylistic analysis, but also based on documentary evidence. He found that the work had originally hung in the Florentine basilica of Santa Maria Maggiore, where it had arrived on January 20th 1474 to be placed on a pillar in the nave. The record of its existence vanishes shortly afterwards, however, if we are to believe that Vasari overlooks it even in the second edition of the Lives (1568); its description is also missing from other records about the church.

According to one theory, Sandro was inspired to paint his Saint Sebastian by an analogous but smaller panel on the same theme, today preserved in the Metropolitan Museum of New York and traditionally attributed to Andrea del Castagno. Later studies however have assigned it to Francesco Botticini, therefore indirectly turning the story of inspiration on its head: the original version must have been Sandro's work.The image of the saint – with his serene face, erect and composed posture – doesn't seem in the slightest troubled by physical pain: it is almost the icon of a hero or pagan god. It is also a virtually disembodied image, framed in a light which comes from all directions. The landscape in the distance, topped by a remote sky, resounds with the recent lessons of the Flemish masters. The background's details are fascinating: the executioners on the left turn away; one of them, at the rear of the group, has just struck a bird with an arrow; closer to the viewer, in a valley, a semi-reclined man looks up at the saint; on the horizon we see the Gothic lines of a classical city of Flanders. Upon closer inspection, however, one realises that the background's function is anything but decorative: the landscape is "cut on all sides by oblique lines, that diverge, or make zig-zags... which guide the diffused light of the horizon towards the saint, through oblique and crossed rays; and that multiplicity of guiding lines of perspective and light is reiterated in the arrows buried in the figure itself. So the light, coming from different directions and at different times, strikes a body that does not exist nor insist in a defined space; and which, rendered transparent by the opposing rays, is not even solid" (Argan).

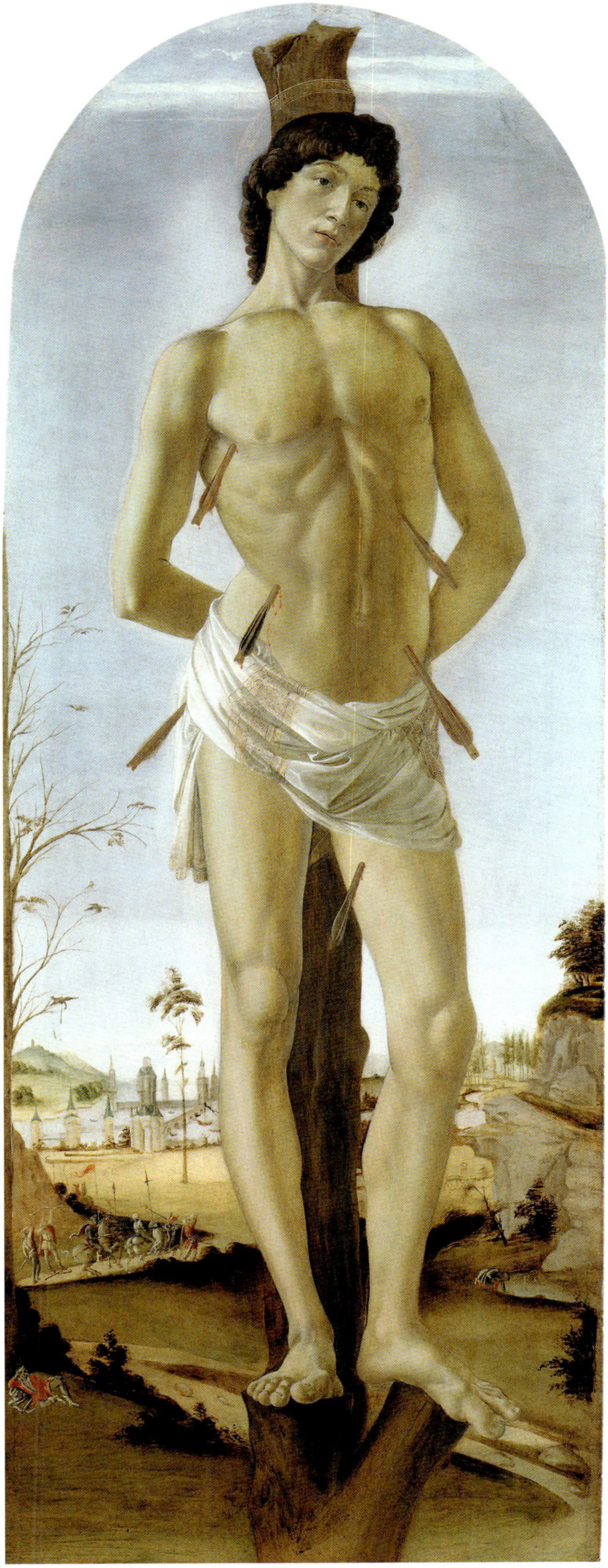

Paris

Musée du Louvre

The Villa Lemmi frescos

Villa Lemmi, a property in Careggi near Florence, embodies the evolution of a fortified country estate built in remote times. During the first half of the fifteenth century it passed from the Ginori to the Da Galliano clan, a family of minor nobility from Mugello, before being transferred to Giovanni di Francesco Tornabuoni in 1469. The brother of Lucrezia, wife of Piero de' Medici ditto il Gottoso, Giovanni was the maternal uncle of Lorenzo il Magnifico and took on the role of treasurer to Pope Sixtus IV: in this position he was responsible for the work of mediation which led to the involvement of the Florentine artists in the Sistine Chapel in 1480 (see p. 50).

The villa also passed into many other hands: its current name is actually that of the family that owned it when the Botticelli frescos were uncovered. The discovery dates back to 1873; while restoring the balcony on the second floor, some ancient frescoes emerged from under the old plaster. The paintings were situated on two opposing walls, one on the side of the courtyard, the second on the outside, facing towards the hills of Careggi. Originally, the fresco cycle was perhaps more extensive than the three scenes which were retrieved, the first of which (and the only reproduced here because of its superior clarity) shows a young man before the assembly of the Arts. The second is of Venus, who, accompanied by the Graces, presents gifts to a young woman; the third one is of a male figure who has remained headless, dressed in red, against the backdrop of a river landscape. The first two frescoes which were best preserved, were removed and sold to an antique dealer who then sold them to the Louvre; the third, in poor condition, remained on site.

The authorship of the paintings was immediately attributed to Botticelli, and has never been challenged. The real problem concerns the identification of the characters portrayed. The event celebrated in the cycle is definitely a marriage; and at first was assumed to be the nuptials of Lorenzo Tornabuoni and Giovanna Albizzi, celebrated in 1486. However, some scholars say that the wife in the second fresco looks nothing like Giovanna, of whom there are two portraits by Ghirlandaio: one on panel dating from 1488 (Madrid, museo Thyssen-Bornemisza), and another in the *Visitation* fresco (1489-90) from Santa Maria Novella. The figure of the young woman in fact seems to correspond to the central character in the group of three that follow Giovanna in the *Visitation*: this would be Alessandra, the daughter of Niccolò Tornabuoni and Giovanna's cousin. In fact, in the fresco by Botticelli and the work of Ghirlandaio, the two young women are identical in terms of the hairstyle, veil and pearl necklace with pendant that they both wear. The groom would then be one of the Albizzi clan, Matteo di Andrea, born in 1459. The date of their marriage is unknown, but as the first son of Giovanna and Matteo was born in 1485, we can place it around 1483.

Ernst Gombrich's rather intriguing theory suggests that the Villa Lemmi is not that of the Tornabuoni clan, but rather the villa which Lorenzo di Pierfrancesco de' Medici bought on the occasion of his marriage to Semiramide Appiani (the daughter of Jacopo III, Lord of Piombino) celebrated in 1482. This theory scarcely alters the dating of the frescoes, but interprets them in a radically different manner; i.e, as an allegory of attaining the higher life under the sign of Venus. For Gombrich, the goddess represents the *Humanitas* of the Medici humanism, who separated the senses and material goods from spiritual values; the three Graces that accompany her would be the three aspects of *Liberalitas*, namely *Castitas*, *Pulchritudo* and *Amor*. For Lightbown, the two paintings evoke the cultural education which was granted the offspring of the Florentine oligarchy during the humanist era, when an expertise in finance and literary competence were placed on the same level. A reader of the classics, the young man in the first fresco would be introduced by Grammar – who could solve textual difficulties – into the presence of the other liberal arts and their queen, Prudence; on the right of whom, by small coincidence, sits Arithmetic, an indispensable instrument for bankers and merchants.

A young man before the assembly of the Liberal Arts
1482-83, detached fresco, 237 x 269 cm

This painting is missing large parts at the bottom. The scene takes place at night, perhaps because, according to a tradition found in medieval literature, an encounter between a human and an allegorical figure could only take place in a dream. The young man, wearing a long robe with a cap on his head and a white handkerchief in his right hand, leaves a "dark wood" (ignorance?) and a girl leads him by the hand into the assembly of the Liberal Arts. Their representation is that which is still used today, which was established in the Middle Ages: we have the linguistic and philosophical disciplines of the *Trivium* (Grammar, Rhetoric and Dialectic) and the precise disciplines of the *Quadrivium* (Arithmetic, Geometry, Astronomy and Music). The guiding figure has been interpreted in various ways. Some believe it to be Grammar, and identify Prudence as the woman, seated high up, who chairs the forum; for others the girl who introduces the young man is Minerva, while the other is Rhetoric. The symbolic significance of the handkerchief remains a mystery, but its presence cannot be random as it reoccurs in the hands of the bride in the next scene. Bottom left, a cherub holding a noble coat of arms was lost because it was not painted on wet; it must have been added dry in tempera, and at the moment of discovery, came away along with the plaster.

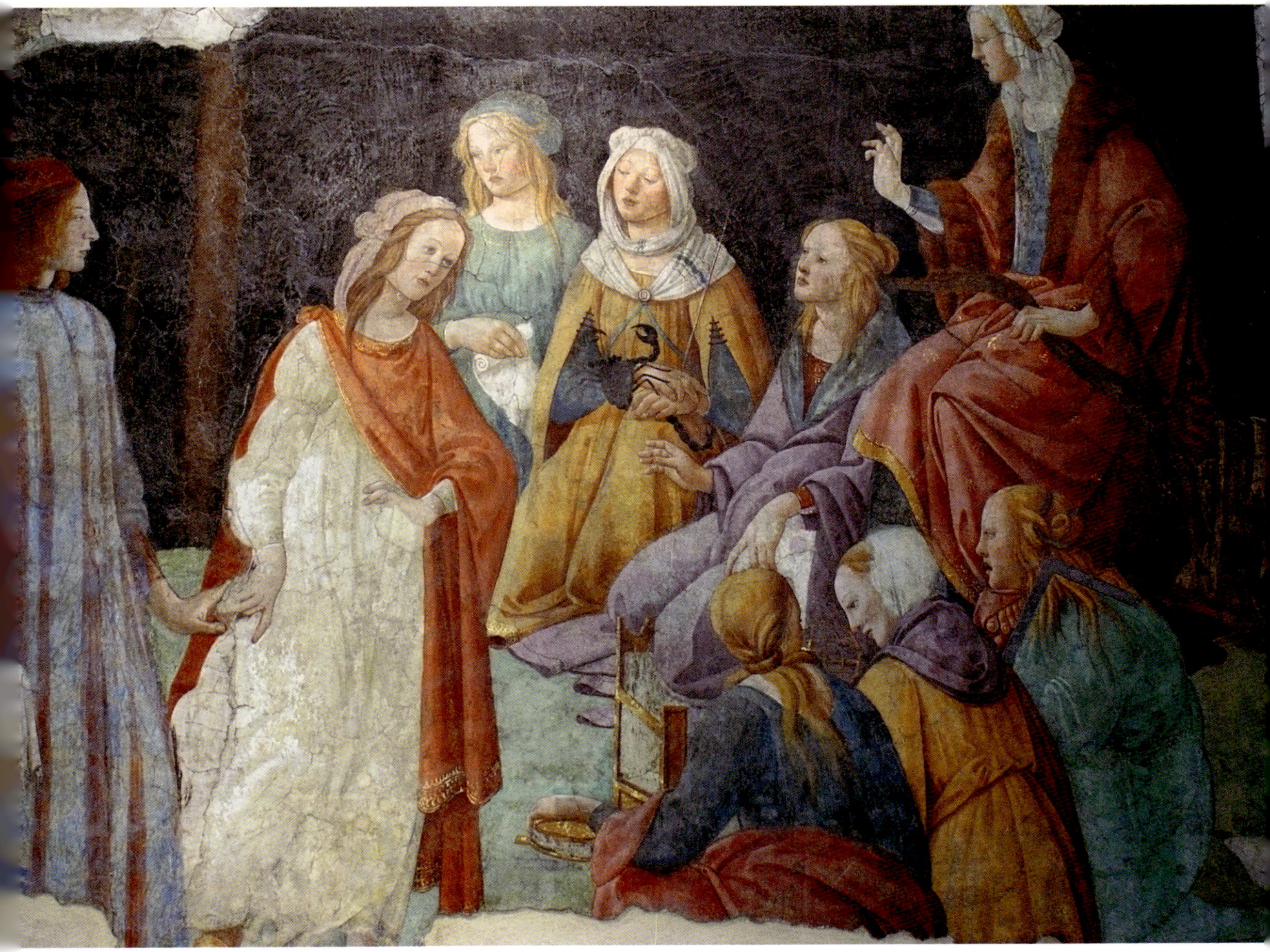

Madrid

Museo Nacional del Prado

The stories of Nastagio degli Onesti

These four panels were painted for the marriage of Giannozzo Pucci and Lucrezia di Piero di Giovanni Bini, which took place around 1483. The sponsor is also significant; the central position of the Medici coat of arms on the third painting stands for Lorenzo il Magnifico, who would have stepped in to arrange the marriage, as Lucrezia Bini was his niece. The four works remained in the house of the Pucci clan – where they were seen by Vasari – until 1868, when a collector from London bought them, and after several changes of hand the last private owner, a Parisian by the name of Spiridion, sold the first three to the Prado. The fourth – which showed up in 1978, according to Mandel, in an American private collection – is now back in possession of the Pucci family.

These were *spalliere* or backboards, both decorative objects and a form of thermal insulation, because in the winter they blocked the moisture seeping from the walls. Under this dual function, they represented a typical wedding gift amongst well-off families, and their subjects usually echoed the theme of marriage and were often derived from Greek and Roman mythology. Here, however, the story told comes from a modern author, Boccaccio, and contains rather dire implications, auspicious in nature only by means of its happy ending. Day V of the *Decameron* contains stories of lovers who find happiness only after "grief or unfortunate accidents". The protagonist of the eighth tale is a young man from Ravenna, Nastagio degli Onesti, who is madly in love with a girl from the noble Traversari family. Nastagio is rich and prepared to do anything to please the girl, but she rejects his courtship. Since the young man is in danger of ruin, his relatives beg him to leave the city; he agrees, going to reside in the nearby pine forest of Chiassi.

As a distraction, he takes his liveliest friends with him; but at one point, seized by nostalgia for his beloved, he walks out into the pine forest and wanders there for some time. Suddenly he hears a woman screaming, and a naked girl runs out before him, followed by two mastiffs biting at her heels; behind them comes a darkly dressed knight, who chases her with his sword raised. Nastagio grabs a tree branch to defend her, but the rider persuades him to desist and tells him his story. His name is Guido of Anastagi, and he explains that he was even more in love with that girl than Nastagio is with his beloved. But driven to desperation by her refusals, he killed himself with the very sword he holds in his hands; shortly after, the pitiless girl had also died. In Hell, they had been condemned to a terrible fate: Guido has to chase the woman, capture her, rip out her heart and give it to the dogs. Straight after, however, she returns to life and the terrible pursuit resumes again; the atrocious episode was destined to repeat itself for as many years as had been the months of suffering inflicted on Guido. The drama took place on fixed days in the same place: precisely there, in the pine forest, every Friday.

On returning to their tents, Nastagio asks his friends to organise a banquet for the following Friday, inviting several acquaintances, including the Traversari clan. In order to win his beloved, he arranges for the women's table to be placed exactly in the spot where Guido's chase will reach its dreadful end. Everything goes to plan, and Nastagio's beloved, suddenly aware "of the cruelty which she has always shown Nastagio… finds her hate transformed into love, and sends her maid secretly to Nastagio". The girl tells the young man that her mistress is willing to give herself unconditionally to him, but Nastagio in knightly fashion responds that he aspires only to marriage. And so it happens. The backboards are, in part, a product of Botticelli's workshop; this was perfectly normal, as commissions for wedding gifts usually involved very little notice. While they were undoubtedly conceived and designed by Sandro, they would have been painted by one or more of his collaborators; for *The wedding breakfast of Nastagio*, in particular, Mandel has suggested the name of Jacopo del Sellaio (1442-1493). Berenson attributes the third, namely *The banquet in the pine forest*, to Bartolomeo di Giovanni (1475-1511), a specialist in "minute detail" who collaborated with the workshops of Ghirlandaio and Botticelli. In any case, the painters must have worked side by side, because the clothing, accessories and backdrops are characterised by an absolute homogeneity. Of the four scenes in which the story is told (*The vision of Nastagio, Guido degli Anastagi rips out the heart of his beloved, The banquet in the pine forest* and *The wedding breakfast of Nastagio*) we present here the first and third, favoured slightly more for their compositional skill and dramatic intensity.

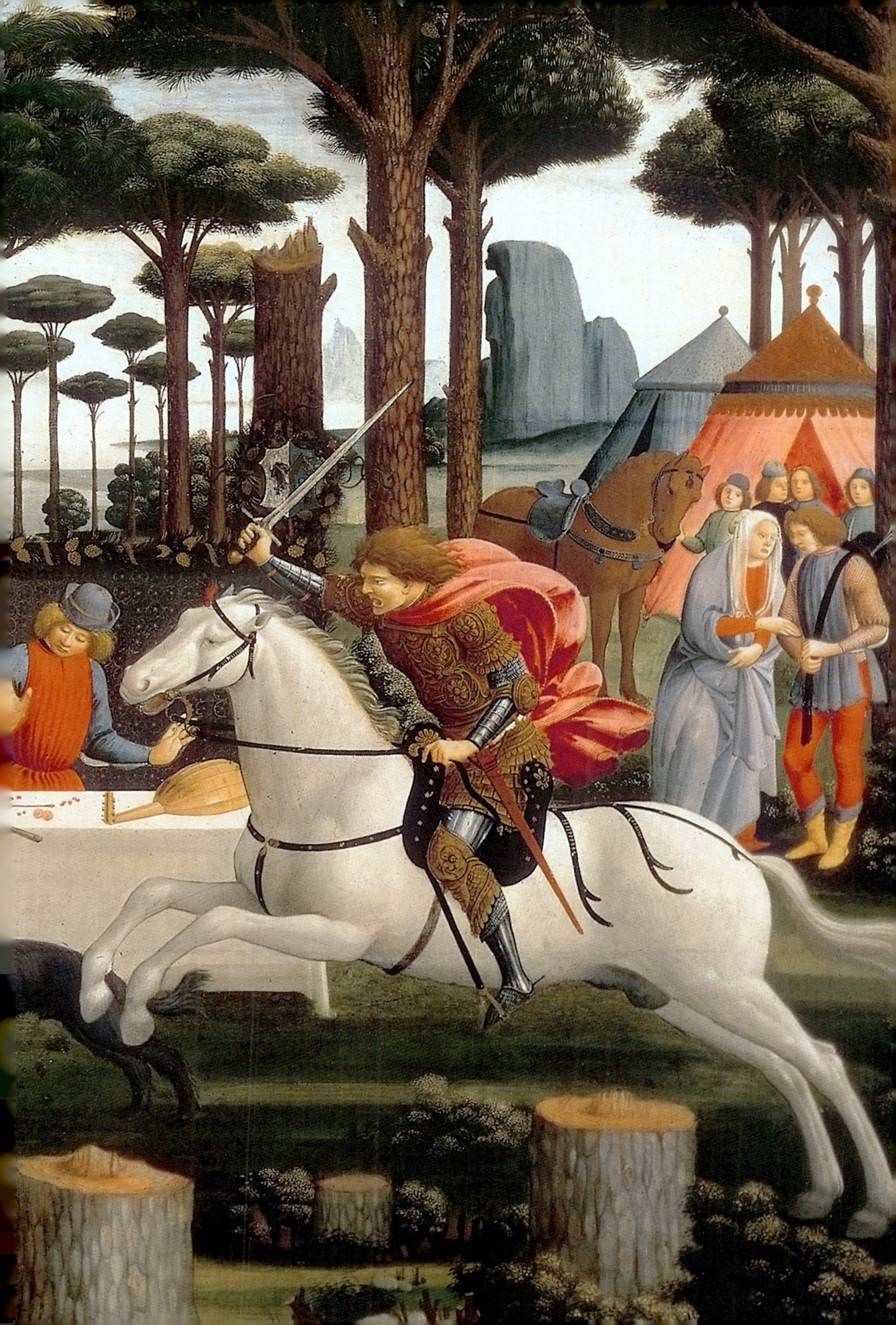

THE VISION OF NASTAGIO
1483, tempera on panel, 83 x 138 cm

This painting simultaneously presents two scenes which are actually distinct, even if they take place in rapid succession. The backdrop for both is the pine forest of Chiassi, which opens onto a bay encircled by the ocean and scored by vessels. In the first episode Nastagio, straying from the tents where he and his friends are staying (we partially see one and the others far left), wanders weighed down by his thoughts, lost in his dream of love. In the second, the young man is shown while grabbing a branch to defend the unhappy maiden chased by Guido degli Anastagi and his mastiffs. The panel scrupulously follows the indication of the literary text, except for one particular: the knight, whom Boccaccio describes as "dark", i.e. dressed in black, has little of the infernal apparition about him; in fact, his shining armour and red cloak rather make us think of St. George.
This unconscious interruption of an object of religious iconography in a tale of pagan origins is far from rare in the painting of the early and middle Renaissance; if we only limit our observations to Botticelli, its enough to recall the central figure of the *Primavera*, whom the critics have often likened to the Madonna.

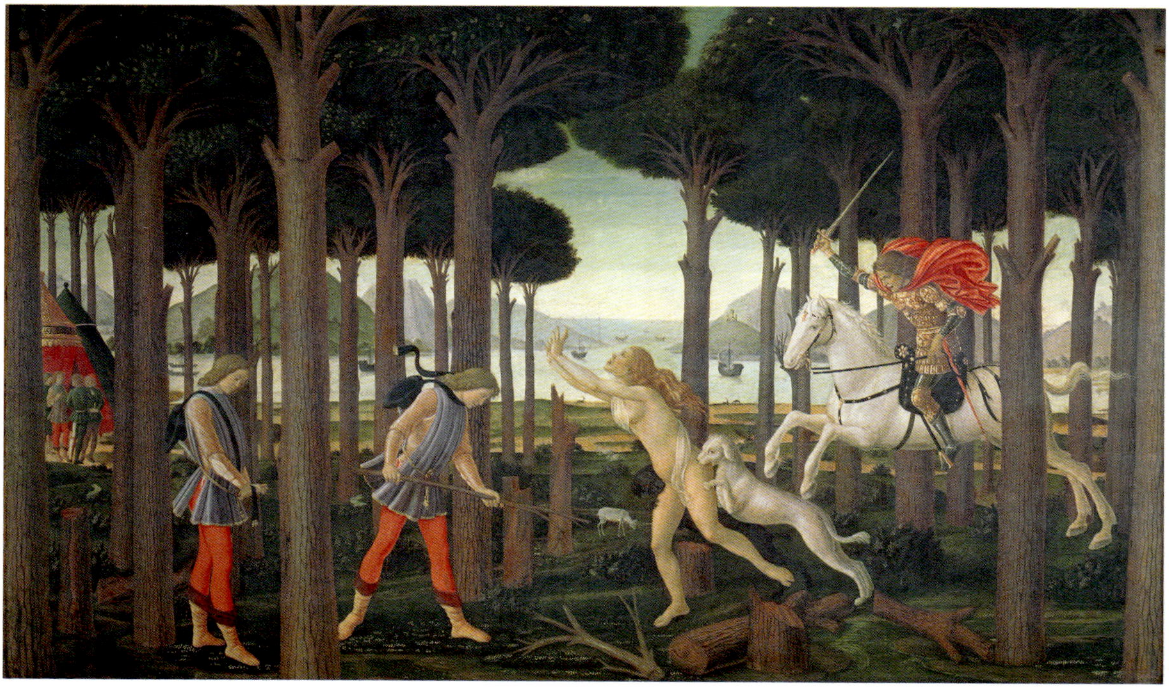

THE BANQUET IN THE PINE FOREST
1483, tempera on panel, 84 x 142 cm

Nastagio decides to throw a banquet on the day in which Guido degli Anastagi has said that the terrible apparition will happen again; he has taken care to position the table of the women to receive the greatest impact of the cruel spectacle. While this takes place, he explains its significance to the guests (*left*). Profoundly moved, the Traversari girl sends her maid to talk with Nastagio (*far right*) to tell him that she is prepared to do anything for the young man. There are three crests on the pine trees that cast shade over the scene; on the left, that of the Pucci family "on a silver field a natural moor's head with a band of silver containing three black Ts", at the centre, that of the Medici clan (the heraldic balls - whose number varied between 12, eight and six – amount to seven in this period), on the right, the Pucci coat of arms quartered with the Bini crest ("on an azure field, a golden square between two roses and a pyramid with six golden hills"), to indicate the wedding of a member of the Pucci family with a Bini. The figure dressed in black, on the far left of the table of the men, has been identified as the father of the groom, Antonio Pucci, while the man with the red hat under the Medici insignia would be the bride's father, Pierfrancesco Bini.

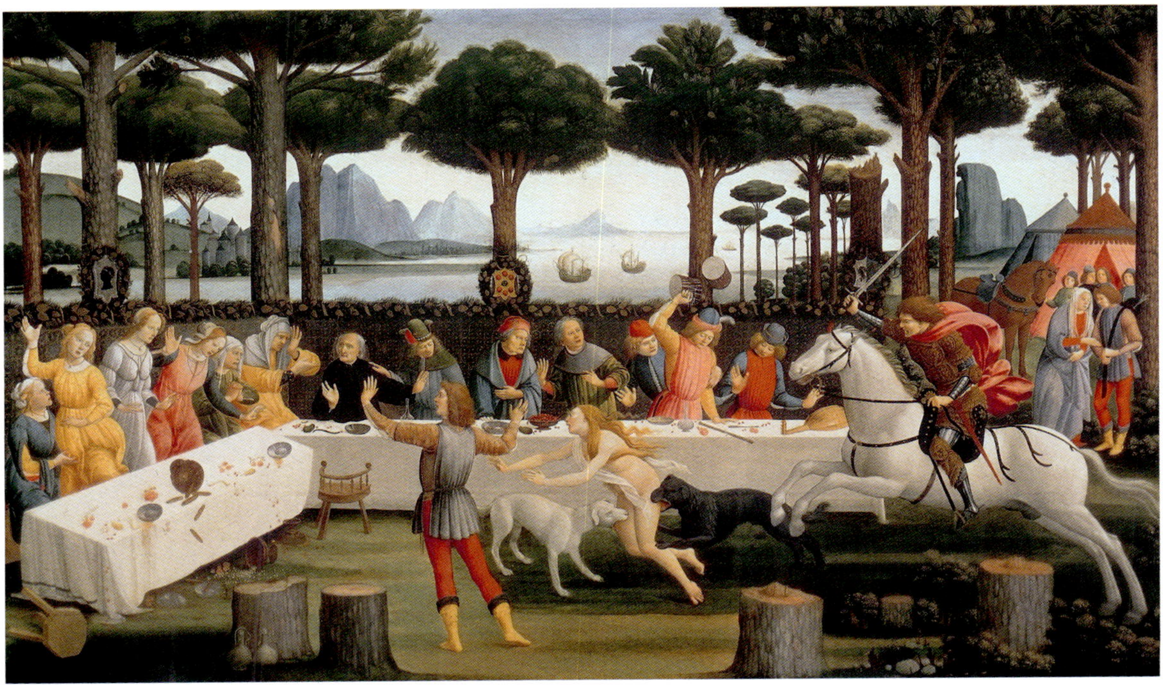

Boston

Isabella Stewart Gardner Museum

Madonna with Child and an Angel Offering Grapes and Wheat
1472, tempera on panel, 85.2 x 65 cm

On account of its symbolic content, this youthful masterpiece by Sandro is known as the *Virgin of the Eucharist*; but also as the *Chigi Madonna*, from the name of the family originally from Sienna which kept the painting in their Roman home until 1899, when the work moved to Boston.
The Virgin, with the Child on her knee, sits before a high balustrade which opens towards the landscape in the background; on her left, an angel crowned with myrtle (attributed to angels and archangels) brings her a cluster of grapes and ears of wheat. The delicate gesture with which the Madonna pulls out a piece of corn is followed by the gaze of the Child, who raises his hand in sign of benediction.
Grapes and wheat have the obvious symbolic significance as the sources of bread and wine, which in the Eucharistic sacrifice are transformed into the body and blood of Christ. But the foreshadowing of the act of sacrifice is also expressly hinted at in the sweet melancholy and knowing gaze of the faces, with lowered eyelids, and the shadow of a smile which expresses a kind of serene acceptance of the divine will.
The extraordinary beauty of the Virgin's face, which is highly legitimate in the overall context of the work, has perhaps inspired those who have suggested a philosophical interpretation, recalling the Neo-Platonic theory of Marsilio Ficino which states that physical beauty is the first step towards divine perfection.
In the painting we find a number of motifs which return in the later painting of Sandro; in particular, the landscape in the background, with its twisting river which anticipates the *Madonna of the Magnificat*. But the most characteristic thing about this work is its momentary alignment with the style of Verrocchio. On the departure of his master Filippo Lippi for Spoleto in 1467, it's probable that Botticelli spent an important period of time in the workshop of Andrea. Some brief comparisons seem to support this hypothesis: the head of the Chigi Madonna has surprising similarities with Verrocchio's Virgin in the Metropolitan Museum of Art in New York, which dates to around 1470; and the face of the angel "with the ghost of a smile, that fleeting and enigmatic expression" (Nicoletta Pons) displays characteristics which are typical of the art of Verrocchio.

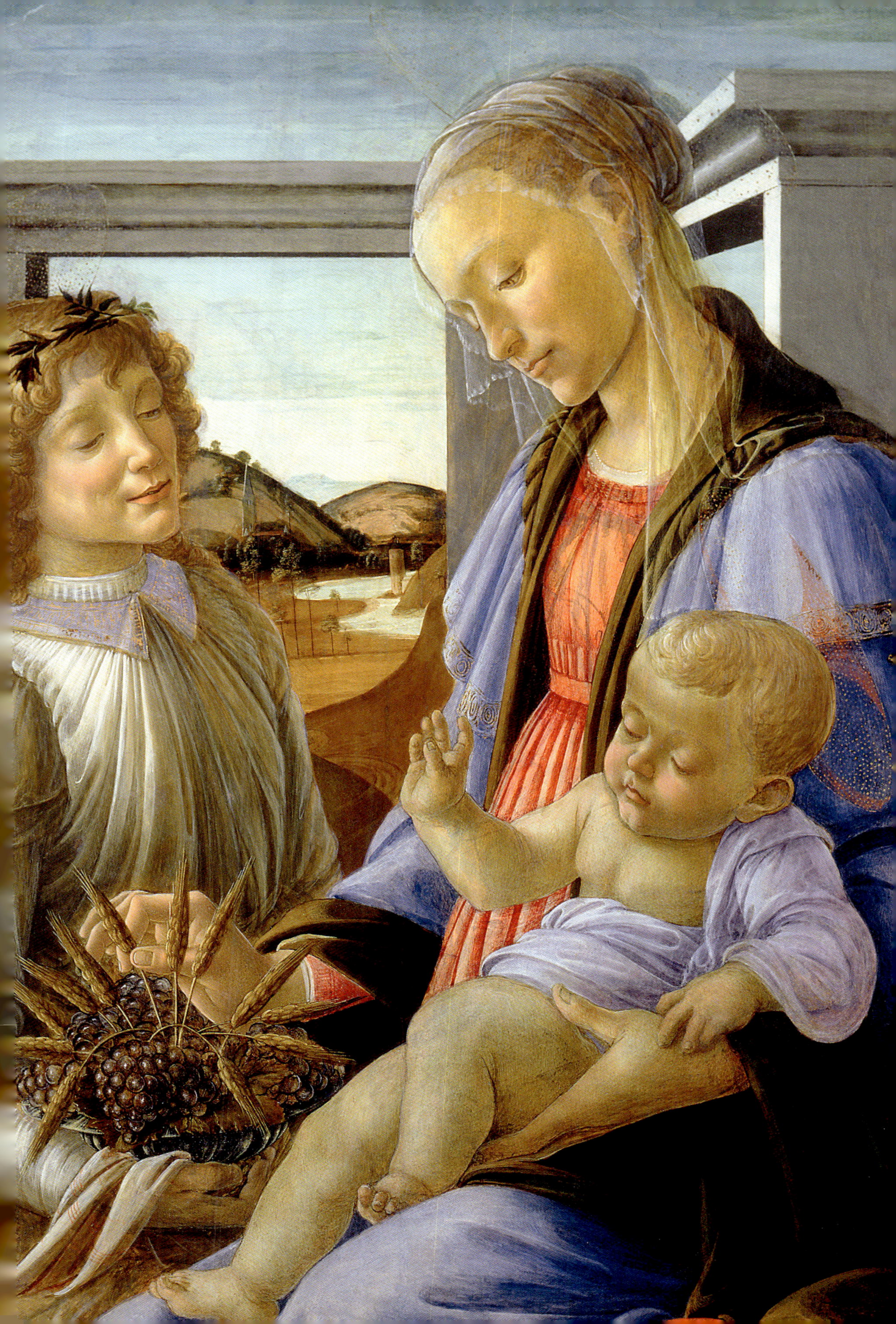

Washington

National Gallery of Art

Adoration of the Magi
1481-82, tempera on panel, 70.2 x 104.2 cm

This panel was purchased in Rome by a French engraver, who in 1808 resold it to the Hermitage in St. Petersburg. It was considered a work of Mantegna, but by 1864, the attribution has passed to Botticelli, and subsequent critics have largely kept the same opinion. In 1933, when the USSR placed it up for sale, it became part of the Mellon collection and finally, by way of inheritance, passed into the collection of the National Gallery. One of the most reliable ancient sources on the work of Sandro, the so-called Anonimo Gaddiano, mentions an *Adoration of the Magi* executed in Rome. A number of elements identify that work with this painting, including iconographic details (the oaks were the heraldic symbol of the della Rovere clan) and stylistic concerns (there are a number of hints of the style of Signorelli and Perugino, whom by coincidence worked side by side with Sandro on the Sistine chapel). Other legacies of his Roman period would include, on the background to the right, the figure of the squire that holds back the horse, for whom Sandro perhaps has in mind the classical sculptural group of the Dioscuri. Of Florentine inspiration, on the other hand, is perhaps the *chiaroscuro*, which is abnormally accentuated here in comparison to Botticellian norms: it's perhaps no coincidence that in 1481 Leonardo undertook his own *Adoration of the Magi*, revolutionary precisely because of its use of *chiaroscuro*, and it was probable that Sandro had seen the sketch before leaving for Rome. Another similarity to the work of Leonardo lies in the fact that the figures of the Virgin and the Child come to represent the undisputed primary focal point, around which all the other figures assume a role of mere embellishment. As in the "Medici" *Adoration* of Santa Maria Novella, the characters are placed in a semi-circle; but here the semi-circle is open towards the spectator, allowing the Virgin to remain totally accessible to the contemplative gaze of all present. What is more, every pose and every gesture are directed towards the Virgin, conferring a new kind of dramatic coherence on the composition. In *De picture* Alberti prescribed the maximum variety both in the execution of the emotions of characters, just as in the representation of their ages and looks, as well as in the portrayal of their perspective: Sandro remains faithful to these dictates, without losing sight of the unifying character of the composition.

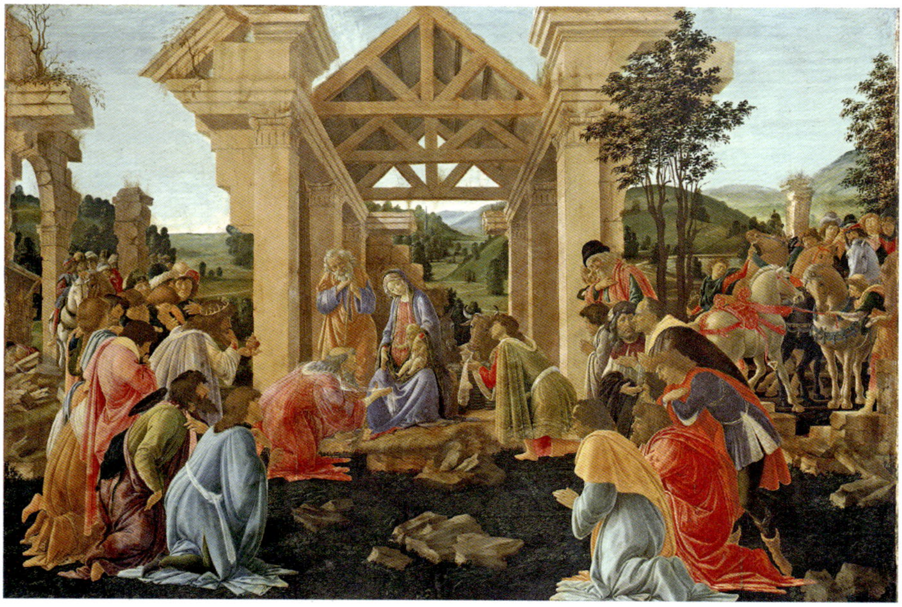

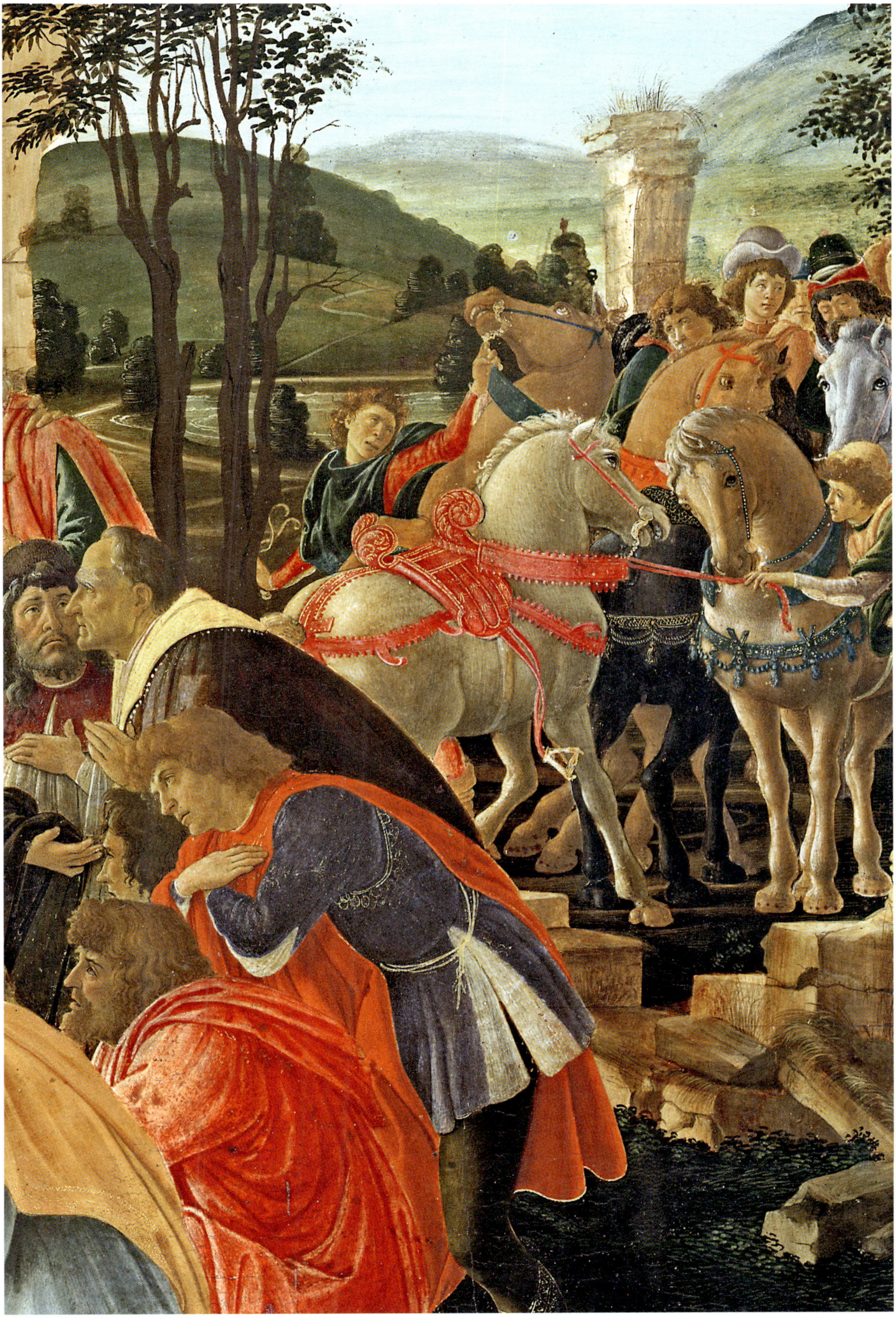

Essential Bibliography

AA.VV., *Botticelli e Filippino. L'inquietudine e la grazia nella pittura fiorentina del Quattrocento*, catalogue from the exhibition at Palazzo Strozzi in Florence, Milan, Skira, 2003; C. ACIDINI LUCHINAT, *Botticelli. Allegorie*, Milan, Mondadori Electa, 2004; G.C. ARGAN, *Botticelli*, Geneva-Paris-New York, Skira, 1957; P.L. CANO ALONSO - J. MARTÍNEZ GÁZQUEZ, *Sobre textos clásicos y pintura: algunas observaciones*, in: "Methodos" (riv. online), Barcelona, 2001; A. CECCHI, *Botticelli*, Milan, Motta, 2005 (series "I grandi Libri d'Arte") —, *Botticelli e l'età di Lorenzo il Magnifico*, Florence, E-ducation.it, 2007 (series "I grandi maestri dell'arte. L'artista e il suo tempo"); —, *Botticelli*, Milan, Motta, 2008 (series "Le Gemme"); E.H. GOMBRICH, *Symbolic Images. Studies in the Art of the Renaissance*, London, Phaidon, 1972; H.P. HORNE, *Alessandro Filipepi, commonly called Sandro Botticelli, painter of Florence*, London, George Bell & Sons, MDCCCCVIII (trad it.: *Alessandro Filipepi detto Sandro Botticelli, pittore in Firenze*, Florence, SPES, MDCCCCLXXXVI); R. LIGHTBOWN, *Botticelli*, Milan, Rizzoli, 1989; S. MALAGUZZI, *Botticelli. L'artista e le opere*, Florence, Giunti, 2004; G. MANDEL (a cura di), *Botticelli. L'opera completa*, present. di Carlo Bo, Milan, Rizzoli, coll. "I classici dell'Arte", 1978; S. MELTZOFF, *Botticelli, Signorelli and Savonarola. "Theologia" poetica and painting from Boccaccio to Poliziano*, Florence, Olschki, 1987; G. REALE - E. SGARBI, *Le nozze nascoste o La Primavera di Sandro Botticelli*, Milan, Bompiani, 2007; R. SALVINI, *Tutta la pittura del Botticelli*, Milan, Rizzoli, 1958; A. WARBURG, *Botticelli*, Milan, Abscondita, 2003.

Note on the author

Carlo Montrésor is the pseudonym of Alberto Anichini. A Florentine historian of the philosophy of education, he has always pursued his work as an editorial professional alongside that of translator, curator and author. In the historical / artistic field, as well as taking responsibility for realising the catalogues for a series of great exhibitions (*André Masson, Florence, Palazzo di Orsanmichele*, 1981; *Arte Maestra da Monet a Picasso, cento capolavori dalla Galleria Nazionale di Praga*, Florence, Palazzo Pitti, 1982; *Arte e Storia in Santa Maria Novella*, museum catalogue, Florence, 1982; *Urbino e le Marche prima e dopo Raffaello*, Urbino, Palazzo Ducale, 1983), he has also collaborated with various publications and produced many guides for Electa (*Guida artistica d'Italia*, 1991; *Le chiese di Venezia*, 1991; *La cattedrale di Ferrara*, 1992; *La cappella degli Scrovegni a Padova*, 1992; *Il palazzo Comunale di Cremona*, 1993), Mandragora (*Firenze. Guida per il viaggiatore curioso*, 1998; *Il Museo dell'Opera del Duomo di Firenze*, 2001) and Becocci (*Scoprire e conoscere Firenze*, 2004). In the context of an initiative between Electa and the weekly publication "Oggi", he also produced a series of monographs on great artists throughout history ("I pocket dell'Arte", 1992). For Electa-Gallimard he has also translated and produced the monograph *Matisse, uno splendore inaudito* (1994) and *Picasso, La ricerca e la memoria* (1995).

Ats Italia Editrice s.r.l.
via di Brava, 41/43 - 00163 Roma
www.atsitalia.it

Text: *Carlo Montrésor*
Editorial co-ordination: *Frida Giannini*
Photo research: *Angela Giommi*
Graphic design, layout and cover: Brenda Maroni (*ATS Italia Editrice*)
Scanning and colour correction: *Leandro Ricci*
Technical co-ordination: *Flavio Zancla*
Translation: *Isobel Lee*
Printing: *Papergraf - Piazzola sul Brenta (PD)*
Photographs:
- PhotoService Electa, Milano
- Archivio Foto Scala, Firenze
- Archivio Rabatti e Domingie, Firenze
- Pag. 77: Madonna and Child with an Angel, c.1472-75 (tempera on panel) by Botticelli, Sandro (1444/5-1510)

ISBN 978-88-6524-111-0